In this book Katherine Kearns explores the feminist, theoretical, and psychoanalytic implications inherent in the relationship between history and narrative. She poses a feminist challenge to the hidden assumptions within conventional historiography by focusing on the troubled relationship between subjectivity and history. By applying Freud's theories of how adult authority is forged, especially his notion of the Oedipus Complex, Kearns considers the anti-feminist, anti-individualist implications of any fully oedipalized discourse. While recognizing the principle that history always occurs within a shared social context, Kearns explores the disguised positivisms that remain embedded within conventional historiographic procedures, and reveals their implications for feminist discourse. The study of history, she argues, whether literary, political, or social, must take us beyond traditionally defined historical contexts to include individual psychological moments and states in which thought and action occur. This is the first book to challenge conventional notions of legitimation, authority and evidence in historical and literary narratives from a feminist perspective.

Psychoanalysis, historiography, and feminist theory

Literature, Culture, Theory 25

❖❖

General editor

RICHARD MACKSEY, *The Johns Hopkins University*

Selected series titles

Psychoanalysis, historiography, and feminist theory

The search for critical method

KATHERINE KEARNS

Whitney Humanities Center
Yale University

CAMBRIDGE
UNIVERSITY PRESS

PUBLISHED BY THE PRESS SYNDICATE OF THE UNIVERSITY OF CAMBRIDGE
The Pitt Building, Trumpington Street, Cambridge CB2 1RP

CAMBRIDGE UNIVERSITY PRESS
The Edinburgh Building, Cambridge CB2 2RU, United Kingdom
40 West 20th Street, New York, NY 10011-4211, USA
10 Stamford Road, Oakleigh, Melbourne 3166, Australia

First published 1997

Printed in the United Kingdom at the University Press, Cambridge

Typeset in 10/12½ Palatino

A catalogue record for this book is available from the British Library

Library of Congress cataloguing in publication data

Kearns, Katherine.
Psychoanalysis, historiography, and feminist theory: the search for critical
method / Katherine Kearns.
p.   cm. – (Literature, culture, theory: 25)
Includes index.
ISBN 0 521 58298 9 (hardback) – ISBN 0 521 58754 9 (paperback)
1. Historiography.   2. History – Philosophy.   3. Psychoanalysis and
feminism.   4. Feminist theory.   I. Title.   II. Series.
D13.K35   1997
907'.2–dc21   97–47372   CIP

ISBN 0 521 58298 9 hardback
ISBN 0 521 58754 9 paperback

VN

For my sons and for my father

Contents

Acknowledgments

This book was begun and completed in a quiet second-floor office in the Whitney Humanities Center at Yale University. I would like to thank David Bromwich, past Director of the Center, and David Marshall, the present Director, for awarding me the Richardson Fellowship that allowed for a full year's freedom from the responsibilities of teaching and departmental life. The Whitney Humanities Center itself, with its rich interdisciplinary life, its conferences, weekly Fellows' meetings, lectures, and seminars, has provided the best possible environment for thinking through disciplinary and methodological expectations. The Yale library collections are, of course, unparalleled, and I am acutely appreciative of the staff members who make the system work and of the bibliographers, among them Margaret Powell and Sue Roberts, who make certain that the collections remain pre-eminent. It is a delicate proposition to thank someone who will, I think, disagree with the most basic premises of my argument, but I feel that I must also recognize Peter Gay, whose National Endowment for the Humanities Seminar on history and psychoanalysis wakened me to the questions this book works to address. Professor Gay, who deserves absolutely none of the blame for this project, provided the atmosphere of free inquiry that made it possible. I would like to thank both Joan Wallach Scott for her early reading of the manuscript and Dominick LaCapra, who, as a reader for Cambridge University Press, made immensely helpful editorial and bibliographic suggestions.

There are many others who have been invaluable in this process.

Acknowledgments

Tom and Jan Samet, John Auchard, Margaret and Hank Powell, Sheila Brewer, Harold Bloom, the Fellows of the Center, copy editor Gillian Maude, my students at Yale and New York University, Grady Ballenger, and my sons, Nicholas and Max, have all contributed to this task, and in more ways than I can name. And finally, with love, I would like to thank my father, Paul Kearns, who is fighting a hard battle with an illness that has almost defeated his body but has left his spirit untouched.

Introduction

'Tell me, Daddy. What is the use of history?'
Marc Bloch, *The Historian's Craft*

PARENTS HAVE BEEN FOUND FOR THE (ORPHAN) UNCONSCIOUS!
Deleuze and Guattari, *Anti-Oedipus*[1]

Methodological homily

Hadrian's Wall, the Great Wall, the Berlin Wall, the Wailing Wall, the Walls of Jericho, the Wall: it is as if History hypostasizes itself in a string of walls across time, as if it entertains a Pharaonic fantasy of permanence, as if it would stop itself, once and for all. As if it might halt the perpetual retreat that defines it. Hitler commissioned the architect Albert Speer to design buildings whose walls would hold against time to stand forever, battered but monumental; even as graceful ruins in the far distant future they would prove that an apotheosis had occurred and a new history written and completed. History, however, did not wait, and the walls came tumbling down. Speer then wrote his history from inside prison walls.

To push to the wall, to go over the wall, to go to the wall: built into the fantasy of stoppage is its opposite, as if the wall is also the hypostasis of a human will that makes history by main force of resistance to its own constructed boundaries. The historian, like the architect Speer with his latter-day Parthenons, must contract to produce a history that will outlast itself; he must construct an edifice that will continue to hold truth over time, even after the temporal specifics of his narrative have been changed into something

---

[1] Gilles Deleuze and Félix Guattari, *Anti-Oedipus: Capitalism and Schizophrenia*, trans. Robert Hurley, Mark Seem, and Helen R. Lane (Minneapolis: University of Minnesota Press, 1989), 79. The capitals here are mine.

1

that makes his work more valuable as 'art' than as 'history,' less a wall for holding up a roof and housing a senate than a wall whose value is in and of itself. The 'permanent cultural predicament,' says Jacques Barzun, is to know how to 'work with the true possibilities of the time, not its verbalisms, if anything solid is to come of its efforts.' 'The task,' he says, 'is to make bricks with the straw supplied to the willing workers.'[2] And not just any straw will do: the fresh stubble, he says, will produce 'insubstantial stuff,' the fancy but fragile building blocks of the theoreticians and the fadists. Only old straw toughened by pitchforks will make bricks that do not crumble with time and a wall that will stand. Solid, everyday language, worked over and tested, square-edged ideas, worked over and tested, a respect for the past, with an educated awareness of its wisdoms and its follies, a preference for the plain stuff of the material world that has been worked over and tested by time so that it transcends its own specific manifestations: Only history can make history, says the historian.

But, says the poet, 'Something there is that doesn't love a wall, / That wants it down.' Something gets into materialities and makes them unpredictable, and, no matter how hard it tries to resist, something gets into language and stirs up its tropological inclinations. The cranky, subversive genius of Frost's 'Mending Wall' is that it celebrates walledness, celebrates the eternally mending wall that refuses to stay put, with its capitulating stones like balls, like loaves, and that also refuses to give up being a wall. The pleasure is in the perversity of the thing; the neither here nor thereness of it makes plenty to do, gives something to talk about, and ensures that its life consists in making itself manifest through change. Frost knows that in poetry, as in love, and as in history, to reach stasis is the same as reaching death. That stone wall marks a place, arbitrary and definitive; language falls on either side, even as the wall itself tumbles to natural forces – frost, ground swells – and to the work of hunters. With the mending wall always more or less there, things can fall into temporary place. Apple trees on one side, pine trees on the other; piously oedipalized neighbor echoing the wisdom of his father on one side ('Good fences make good neighbors') and sentimental ironist on the other. Frost tells the double truths of discursivity in this poem: talk and be mostly

---

[2] Jacques Barzun, *Clio and the Doctors: Psycho-History, Quanto-History, and History* (University of Chicago Press, 1974), x.

misunderstood; go mute and cease to be in the world – within history – , and in love, in any way the world knows how to speak. Yield to the temptations of barrierlessness and lose all formal integrity; escape to within impregnable walls and gain asylum at the expense of selfhood. Speak in the full consciousness of indeterminacy and risk becoming effeminate, being unmanned; yield to the fantasy of having discovered 'the true possibilities of the time, not its verbalisms,' and risk becoming a tyrant rather than the Aristotelian man of moderate virility (the figure after whom the historian patterns himself), a madman rather than a hero. Or put into the Oedipal caricature that informs my own text: give in to the transformative and become inmate Schreber, perpetually becoming a woman, in flux, mad; refuse the same, and become Schreber's father, authoritarian and totalizer. Frost makes it clear that it is good and necessary to rebuild the falling wall, but that it is only the safe, the beautiful, and the eternally frustrating fact of its inevitable capitulations that makes the gesture meaningful. The historian, whose business is to carve permanence out of change, may recognize but cannot celebrate the sheer intransigence of the things – material and linguistic – with which he works.

The precariously stolid wall that acts out its contiguities with air, earth, fire, and water, and with the work of human hands, is Frost's metonymy for an integumental truth whose permanence is the paradox of a transformative (human) nature in resistance to its own mutability; its performance of its clumsily delicate wallness is everything because it keeps dropping meaning into a bottomless hole of possibility. With every Sisyphus who raises a stone back to the top, the cycle begins again. History as a mending wall, then, or a river (another of history's metaphors for itself), with a rock jutting out to mark one's place as a force at once within and in despite of the flow, affected by and affecting the movement around it. 'Existence,' Frost says in 'West-Running Brook,' (he might, as well, have called it 'meaning,' or 'language,' or 'history'):

> It seriously, sadly, runs away
> To fill the abyss's void with emptiness.
> It flows beside us in this water brook,
> But it flows over us. It flows between us
> To separate us for a panic moment.
> It flows between us, over us, and *with* us.
> And it is time, strength, tone, light, life, and love –

> And even substance lapsing unsubstantial;
> The universal cataract of death
> That spends to nothingness – and unresisted,
> Save by some strange resistance in itself,
> Not just a swerving, but a throwing back,
> As if regret were in it and were sacred.

This is a figure for History's double burden of metaphysics and temporality, its necessary sense of an existence whose only material manifestation is in its lapse toward death, but whose ability to apprehend this truth is exactly the thing that, at another level of knowing entirely, refutes it.

Compounded of nihilism and good faith, these poems speak directly, which is to say obliquely, poetically, performatively, to physical and linguistic conditions that baffle the nosologist, the critic, the analyst, and the historian. Freed of the strictures faced by these technicians, the poet can perform the apprehensions that analytic language only fixes in amber things already dead; the poet can remind one of the arbitrary nature of language as regards 'truth.' This text would like to begin by bringing these intuitions to the fore, even as it recognizes the impossibility of keeping them in full play. It would like to resist any effort to be taken unilaterally, even as it would hope to remain comprehensible and compelling as a document within the domain of critical discourse. For a world of reasons that I hope will become gradually persuasive, I would like this text to enact an alternative to the more standard methodological and rhetorical gambits of analytical writing while attaining some of the authority of that mode. As with Frost's most unremarkable and mundane stone wall, I would hope to invest the rather clumsy functionalism of my analysis with enough restless energy to keep the neighbors on their toes.

What follows will work to explain a methodology – and this is already a paradox – whose agenda is to destabilize methodological expectations; this book is an attempt to speak of Oedipal pedagogy without succumbing completely to its lessons, a tricky proposition. This methodological choice mirrors the irony of 'Mending Wall' with its speaker who professes to find wall mending useless even as he calls his neighbor to the task each spring. I want a falling wall, put here precisely to bring out the neighbor, with his father's sayings, for an afternoon's work. Things tug at the wall, and any single answer to the question of causality is merely whimsical,

4

authoritarian, or deluded. Why does it fall? 'I could say 'Elves' to him,' says Frost's speaker, 'But it's not elves exactly, and I'd rather / He said it for himself.' This text would like to evade taxonomy, because to be identified is to be killed off; to be compartmentalized, particularly as a work of 'feminism,' is to guarantee a substantially segregated audience.[3] So it's not elves, exactly, but something wants to keep the wall in motion. And the neighbor?

> I see him there,
> Bringing a stone grasped firmly by the top
> In each hand, like an old-stone savage armed.
> He moves in darkness as it seems to me,
> Not of woods only and the shade of trees.
> He will not go behind his father's saying,
> And he likes having thought of it so well
> He says again, 'Good fences make good neighbors.'

Terms

These reflections on what I will call conventional historiography and on psychohistoriography are at one level pragmatic in that they address the problem, for me unsolved and apparently insoluble, of how one legitimizes an argument; at another level they involve the questions a literary critic asks about how language works – how it enacts a reciprocal effect on the user, how texts create their own imperatives and dictate certain responses, how tropological energies enter the equation when the textual purposes are avowedly other than fictional or poetic. These are ideological stakes, inextricably bound up here with something that can be called, for short, 'feminism.' A random reading of psychohistory will bring into consciousness an awareness that conventional historiography more usually preempts with silence: the oedipalized nature of historical narrative virtually guarantees a reading of evidence that will damn the 'female,' however it is assigned, to insufficiency or excess before the fact. Asleep or awake, passive or active, married or single, childless or progenitive, unattractive or attractive, women get the short end of the Oedipal stick: immersed themselves in Oedipal propaganda, they suffer the weight of the Pontellier Paradox, endure the Witch's Baptism whereby neither sink nor swim will do.

[3] See, for example, Joan Wallach Scott, *Gender and the Politics of History* (New York: Colombia University Press, 1988).

More broadly stated, the stake is 'justice,' a term that demands negotiation and constant, skeptical evaluation if it is to perform with any semantic relevance at all: who may speak, how is the 'real,' so precious a concept to historiography, to be claimed, where is the line between madness and sanity, tutelage and enfranchisement, maleness (power) and femaleness (passivity) to be drawn? Within this domain, where feminism is always implicit within questions of justice, Daniel Paul Schreber is the touchstone; judge and madman, man and woman, he is the living figure of ambiguity, and his ambiguous presence infiltrates this text. His sense of endlessly becoming female, a preoccupation that both he and his evaluators see as among the most crucial evidence of the seriousness of his case, is an image that drives my specifically feminist concerns. Schreber's acute perception of his physical/psychic/spiritual condition as at once fluid and transformative and as under severe constraints (the formalisms of custom and of 'sanity,' the architectural and therapeutic truths of asylum walls) becomes here a figure for both the historian's and the critic's ontological anxieties. His status, at once liminal and institutionalized, writes large the more covert disruptions and superimpositions within normalcy. And his part in the Oedipal drama has a virtually fairytale power; an apparent casualty of the Oedipal contract, he is in his shattered obstinacy both its proof and its refutation. 'Humpty Dumpty sat on a wall / Humpty Dumpty had a great fall.' And neither all the king's horses nor all the king's men could put poor Schreber together again. Schreber, who falls off the Oedipal fence, is historiography's nightmare fantasy.

It should be clear from the beginning that I am willfully avoiding subscription to Freud's theory of the Oedipus Complex as a developmental absolute. I am at the same time acknowledging its considerable explanatory value in speaking of a familiar phenomenon and accepting its role in the naming of, and therefore the consolidation of power in, a masculine dynamic whose source I do not pretend to fathom. Deleuze and Guattari take a definitive position: 'We do not deny that there is an Oedipal sexuality, an Oedipal heterosexuality and homosexuality, an Oedipal castration, as well as complete objects, global images, and specific egos. We deny that these are productions of the unconscious.'[4] This ground

---

[4] Deleuze and Guattari, *Anti-Oedipus: Capitalism and Schizophrenia*, 74.

is admirably staked by the kingly sounding parallelisms of the 'we do not deny/we deny' formulation; mine is necessarily less so, since I am, among other things, wary of the negational energies such definitiveness sets in motion (where 'We do not deny' and 'We deny' also invert themselves). As are they, I am skeptical of taking the 'unconscious' as a deified absence, unknowable and (omni)potent, but I do not *know* that my intuitions are correct. Within the Oedipal dispensation, this uncertainty might be felt as a troubling ambivalence; outside it, it is business as usual, just another everyday pragmatic negotiation.

'Oedipus' becomes in this text a metonymy for what, after Freud, is explicitly articulated as desire channeled by castration anxiety away from home and into the masculine world of work and socialized behaviors; inasmuch as his story takes its power from a specific literary source and inasmuch as it represents itself in part by summing up ample evidence from the historical and literary past, I will use it as a trope for a system of behaviors, linguistic and otherwise, that both precedes and follows Freud's systematizing of it. While I think that the dissemination of Freud's specific assertions make reactions to his claims inevitable, and while I think his theory is, paradoxically, as performative in its effects as it is constative (in speaking itself it generates its terms – resistance or assimilation or a mixture of these modes), I also acknowledge a pre-existent dynamic whose energies may speak multiple languages, a space in which Freud dreamed his model and the terms for his particular story. Jean-Joseph Goux, in *Oedipus, Philosopher*, elaborates on the apprehension that, as he says, 'it is the Oedipus myth that explains the concept.'

In other words, it is within a specific historical institution of subjectivity, within the framework of a particular symbolic mechanism (of which the Oedipus myth is the most powerful manifestation), that something like the 'Oedipus Complex' has been able to command attention and elicit description. It is because the West is Oedipean that Freud discovered the 'Oedipus Complex.' And in this sense, the logic of the Oedipus myth as myth may clarify – or even subvert – Freud's description of the Oedipus 'complex.' This analytic reframing may even give Freud's discovery the possibility of speaking to us, perhaps differently, at a time when historical attrition threatens to nullify the concepts on which it was based.[5]

[5] Jean-Joseph Goux, *Oedipus, Philosopher*, trans. Catherine Porter (Stanford University Press, 1993), 2.

One may respect Freud's attempts to determine first causes and thereby provide explanations of human behavior and remain, nonetheless, skeptical of a story so seductively totalizing and so charmingly capacious. The 'Oedipus Complex' story feels as if it could be one of those famous apocryphal bits of history, like Hamilton's having said, 'Your people, Sir, is a great beast,' or Douglas having held Lincoln's hat at the inauguration, that, having been disproved or gone unsubstantiated, refuses nonetheless to give up its status as necessary truth.[6] Yet such stories, by proving themselves necessarily compelling, further prove themselves to hold a kind of poetic truth, which is to say a truth that in metaphorizing a psychic 'fact' becomes only supplementary to, or a distraction from, history as it is classically defined. The subversive tenacity of the ineffable is enough to make scientists and historians mad; antithetical to history, such 'facts' play themselves out within an interior landscape that, invisible itself, must be articulated through the recognizable topographies of language. Clothed in allegory, these otherwise empty 'facts' compete with, and undermine, the likelihood that one can speak transparently – which is to say, non-metaphorically – about more substantial, measurable externalities. They make poets, where men should be. They raise the unbearable vision of a self shaped entirely from these fancy figures, tattered clothes upon a stick with no substance called 'man' underneath.

The historian's deep anxiety about psychohistory rises up from this shared source, for psychohistory is felt to speak of psychic specters as if they were demonstrable entities, thus blurring the boundary-lines between the felt and the seen, the fictive and the real. Once this happens, the demarcations between history and poetry, history and physiology, history and psychology, history and religion, history and eros, begin to fade, and history threatens to disappear into the language that speaks it. In 'The Ethical Function of the Historian' (1908), David J. Hill makes what is to become a representative statement about the dangers of losing history to disciplines more interested in specific causal theories than in fact: 'If history is ever to throw any light upon the riddle of personality, beyond that which biology and psychology can afford, it can be done in no other way than by bravely pursuing its own method of recording the acts of men as they have actually

---

[6] See Howard K. Beale, 'The Professional Historian: His Theory and His Practice,' *Pacific Historical Review*, 22 (1953), 243.

occurred, and not by elaborating theories of causation.'[7] It is brave – i.e. manly – to wrestle with the tangible, irrefutable facts of daily existence. To give in to more inward struggles, and the more compelling the more they are to be resisted, is to give up being a man, and a historian (Hofstadter, in *Anti-Intellectualism in American Life* [1962], has documented a deep-seated suspicion of intellectuality, as associated with poets, women, invalids, and sissies). 'Oedipus' is a most powerfully troubling story in this context, not because it necessarily tells the 'true story,' but because it so clearly tells a necessary one. *The* necessary one for history, in fact, for it not only lays out the dangers of effaced boundaries, but it enacts the corrective: it is a most viscerally effective pedagogy.

Yet perhaps these kinds of (hi)stories represent the closest one can come to an intuition about 'truth': what feels like a near-brush with the absolute makes closet metaphysicians of us all; the perpetual failure of consummation makes us, at the same time, nihilists, ironists, and skeptics. Still, using the same inchoate material, one might tell other originary myths than the Oedipal; one might start with the linguistic/psychic habit of negation, for example, that doubleness that allows an assertion to hold two oppositional but interdependent truths at once. One could say that, entering into a linguistic field already overdetermined toward misogyny, negation triggers in Freud himself the compensations of the Oedipus Complex theory and explains the primacy of the Oedipal trope in describing processes of ordering and control. In any event, it is questions I am after, more than answers, because the predisposition for, the insistence upon, and the satisfaction with, *answers* constitute the major terms of the Oedipal contract; the need for a template by which chaos might be shaped to order is desire oedipalized into productivity. What is wanted is not more certainty but more ambiguity, room for negotiation. One wants to ask these questions in the hopes that the Oedipal spell might be broken; if some more equitable and less misogynistically performative trope emerges, so much the better.

(Psycho)historiography

I am also aware that in mythologizing traditional or conventional 'historiography' into a more generalized notion than it is in

---

[7] David J. Hill, 'The Ethical Function of the Historian,' *American Historical Review*, 14, 1 (October 1908), 16–17.

practice, the following discussion at one crucial level reproduces the dilemma it seeks to expose; yet this inexorable, seemingly inescapable generating of the paradigmatic over the specific is, ironically enough, one source of my insight into historiography's Oedipal compensations, the source of my anxiety, and the source of my conviction that Oedipal amnesia is all that stands between the historian's notion of truth, evidentially verifiable, and the chaos of multiplicity. My own discussion suffers the historian's double responsibility to retain the truth of discrete particularities within a constructive narrative, and it is plagued with a sense of its own presbyopia, a sense of not being able to see the trees for the forest, a sense that everything is a matter of rack focus, each momentary plane of clarity in any depth of field bought at the expense of blurred surroundings. If historiography is more than ordinarily susceptible to paternal influence, it is not the mere fact of this duress that provokes my own response, then, for who is not under some similar assault by a power, internal and/or external, felt as both painful and comforting? It is instead a sense that the visitation often goes unremarked or unnoticed, or is actively denied by the brotherhood itself, with a sort of Invasion of the Body-Snatchers result.

This suspicion is nothing new at all in the sense that it is at one level a recapitulation of the Nietzschean and Derridean charge of history's complicity with metaphysics: history is, as Derrida has famously said, 'a concept which has always been in complicity with a teleological and eschatological metaphysics, in other words, paradoxically, in complicity with that philosophy of presence to which it was believed history could be opposed.'[8] But I do not mean to focus on the endless game of metaphysical name calling (Nietzsche, claiming himself to be metaphysics-free, calls earlier philosophers metaphysicians; Heidegger, claiming to have exited all metaphysical expectations himself, calls Nietzsche and Sartre metaphysicians and humanism a metaphysics; Rorty, claiming the non-metaphysical status of pragmatism, calls Heidegger a metaphysician, etc. 'Metaphysician,' says one boy to the other. 'I know you are, but what am I?' answers his opponent. 'Metaphysician,' answers the first). Instead of disputing the case, I will

[8] Jacques Derrida, 'Structure, Sign and Play in the Discourse of the Human Sciences,' in *Writing and Difference*, trans. Alan Bass (University of Chicago Press, 1978), 291.

assume the metaphysical bias behind the historian's standard question, 'What is history,' and I will assume a tight link between historiography's ambivalence toward metaphysics (if not at the level of high theory, always at the level of practice) and its reliance upon oedipalized expectations. I will proceed from that (always debatable) assumption to examine the effects of the systemic infiltrations of metaphysics and its metonymously condensed affiliate, the Oedipus story, within historiography of a certain sort.[9] And I will take the Nixonian line for myself: I am not a metaphysician.

So in galvanizing a 'historian' into life, I do so with full recognition both of the Frankensteinian effrontery of the gesture and of the crude approximation it makes to any of the real, elegant, articulate, whimsical historians I know. With R. G. Collingwood's *The Idea of History* as a cautionary guide regarding the complexities of some modern (as opposed to some post-modern) historiographical procedure and thought, as well as proof of the enriched possibilities for a marriage of philosophy and history (and as a paradigmatic case of the covert and ultimately contradictory premises of this perceived co-operation, as well), I have envisioned the figure of the 'conventional historian.' He is made up of found parts, the bits and pieces of several representative men who have given in to the temptation to write *about* historiography. Ranke's toe, Humboldt's ankle, Hegel's knee, Elton's behind, Hexter's wrist, Carr's elbow, Barzun's shoulder, Collingwood's chin, Bloch's brow; Gay's smile. From an historian's point of view, of course, this methodological choice can hardly seem justified, as it is itself in defiance of the

---

[9] See, for a few examples, Peter Gay, *Freud for Historians* (New York: Oxford University Press, 1985); Marc Bloch, *The Historian's Craft*, trans. Peter Putnam (New York: Vintage, 1953); Edward Hallett Carr, *What is History?* (New York: Alfred A. Knopf, 1962); R. G. Collingwood, *The Idea of History*, ed. Jan Van Der Dussen (Oxford: Clarendon Press, 1993). Among other recent or relatively recent books on historiography, see John Higham, *History: Professional Scholarship in America* (Baltimore: Johns Hopkins University Press, 1965); J. H. Hexter, *The History Primer* (New York: Basic Books, 1971); Gertrude Himmelfarb, *The New History and the Old: Critical Essays and Reappraisals* (Cambridge, Mass: Harvard University Press, 1987); Michael Kammen, *Selvages and Biases: The Fabric of History in American Culture* (Ithaca: Cornell University Press, 1975); Peter Novick, *That Noble Dream: The 'Objectivity Question' and the American Historical Profession* (Cambridge University Press, 1988); David J. Russo, *Clio Confused: Troubling Aspects of Historical Study from the perspective of U.S. History* (Westport: Greenwood Press, 1995).

material, temporal, and circumstantial premises by which historiography typically, if sometimes only putatively, operates. For the sake of larger similarities and in an attempt to renegotiate old categories, this grouping willfully puts aside the usual organizational imperatives; it mixes centuries and nationalities, brackets or resists claimed ideological and methodological differences that would, within conventional arrangements, make an 'objectivist' of one man and a 'relativist' of another; on the assumption that the distinction is almost spurious anyway, it mixes philosophical historians and meat and potatoes men (as Hayden White says, 'every historical discourse contains within it a full-blown if only implicit philosophy of history'[10]); on the premise that they are brothers under the skin, it puts psychohistorians and their opponents in the same boat. Yet I have the comfort of a precedent in Peter Gay's *Freud for Historians*, where he says of his own similar move, 'The nervous historian I have invoked and will continue to invoke is a construction, but not a straw man. He is a condensation of many anxious and therefore hostile practitioners who embodies the consensus in the historical craft.'[11] From my point of view such inventions cannot be avoided, even as one always hopes that there is more substance than straw in the figure that emerges (although Dorothy's scarecrow, lamenting his lack of a brain while performing at the level of a wily and inventive pragmatism, would be a figure congenial to the historian's view of himself as a hard-working guild member without philosophical pretensions). Rather than full accountability, the question instead becomes that of the candor with which one admits to a necessarily partial sightedness regarding the evaluation at hand. In both disciplinary modes there is the shared pitfall of necessary reductionisms, the one merely choosing to be less overtly and consciously plagued by the epistemological problem this necessary reductionism represents than the other.

I speak of 'historiography' and 'historians' in a way that I would hope is reasonably representative of a certain ongoing set of assumptions about the discipline. For the most part, I bracket more recent, post-structuralist theories on Barzun's assumption that the history of historiography has proven that 'The pendulum swings. The narrow view begets the desire for breadth, after which the

[10] Hayden White, *Tropics of Discourse: Essay in Cultural Criticism* (Baltimore: Johns Hopkins University Press), 126.   [11] Gay, *Freud for Historians*, 8.

need is felt again for close scrutiny . . . After two or three alternations, the new phase might just as appropriately be called reactionary as progressive.'[12] Barzun's assertion itself may or may not be accurate, although he claims to have history on his side, but the fact that many historians continue to echo his position would suggest that it is accurate enough for the discussion at hand. One also has the sense that the pendulum, historiographic and otherwise, is on the backswing, that this particular moment is charged with 'corrective' impulses back toward a methodological status quo that, inadvertently or not, lends itself to repressed anti-feminist, exclusionary, and anti-intellectual energies.[13] Indeed, mainstream and conservative historians often claim that the new questions outsiders see as having entered historiographical discourse are really not part of historiography proper at all but merely localized contaminations, temporary but nonetheless lamentable and pernicious, from literary criticism, theory, and continental philosophy; the reasoning, whose semantic integrity is actually supported by the history of historiography, is, 'If theory, then not history.'

The 'historian' in this text is neither an avowed realist nor an avowed positivist nor an avowed objectivist, but his assumptions carry some residue of these attitudes regarding material evidence. That is to say, he considers the gathering of detail, the verification of fact, and the accuracy of transmission to be necessary and important, and, more than this, he proceeds with the background faith that these processes will transform his narrative into something more epistemologically legitimated because more externally verifiable, than the fictional narratives with whom it shares its language and format: if not Truth, then truth of a sort, behind which, in the far distance, stands the initiating power, Truth; and if not Human Nature, then human nature of a sort, to which certain ontological assumptions will always apply; and, by extension, if not Humanism, then a particularized and discrete existentialism, located historically, that is (as Sartre has said) a humanism.[14] These faiths may be proclaimed, or they may be qualified,

---

[12] Jacques Barzun, *Clio and the Doctors*, 10.

[13] See Scott, *Gender and the Politics of History*, 15–27; See too, H. Stuart Hughes, 'Contemporary Historiography: Progress, Paradigms, and the Regression toward Positivism,' in *Progress and Its Discontents*, eds. Gabriel A. Almond, Marvin Chodorow, and Roy Harvey Harris (Berkeley, 1982).

[14] See Martin Heidegger, 'Letter on Humanism,' in *Basic Writings*, ed. David Farrell Krell (San Francisco: HarperCollins, 1977), 190–242.

disguised, or deferred, but they remain immanent. As an example, one might take Peter Novick's *That Noble Dream*, which, working to explore the vicissitudes of 'objectivity,' manfully attempts to punch its way out of a paper bag. His good and reasonable intentions – 'The book's aim is to provoke my fellow historians to greater self-consciousness about the nature of our work' – and his historiographic restlessness are conducted from *within* the very terms they interrogate; working inside the standard oppositional structure whose value it would qualify – objectivity/subjectivity, rationalism/irrationalism – the book hopes to situate 'the objectivity question' in the 'stream of history.' Thus its very claim of 'ecumenism' and to the 'overdetermination of all activity, including thought,' rests on certain bedrock assumptions about historicism and the historian's obligations to 'truth,' carefully qualified.[15] Joan Scott speaks in the introduction to *Gender and the Politics of History* of 'things either so taken for granted or so outside customary practice that they are not usually a focus for historians' attention.' 'These include,' she says, 'the notions that history can faithfully document lived reality, that archives are repositories of facts, and that categories like man and woman are transparent.'[16]

My figure has as well what seems to be a fairly common historian's attitude toward written language: as Scott says, the historian believes, or at least resolutely proceeds, as if certain categories are inalienable, and from this follows his conviction that language can be made more or less transparent, a vehicle for communicating facts, details, circumstances, etc., and that it should be kept relatively simple, unadorned, and jargon free for this purpose. For this reason as well as for others, he shares what Hayden White has designated the 'all but universal disdain with which modern historians regard the 'philosophy of history,' of which Hegel is the modern paradigmatic example.'[17] In an earlier swing of the pendulum, George Burton Adams, in his 1909 essay, 'History and the Philosophy of History,' deplores the 'recrudescence of philosophy.' 'Are we passing from an age of investigation to an

---

[15] Peter Novick, *That Noble Dream: The 'Objectivity Question' and the American Historical Profession* (New York: Cambridge University Press, 1988), 7–9, 17.

[16] Scott, *Gender and the Politics of History*, 3.

[17] Hayden White, 'Narrativity in the Representation of Reality,' in *The Content of the Form: Narrative Discourse and Historical Representation*, (Baltimore: Johns Hopkins University Press, 1987), 21.

age of speculation?' he asks; after fifty years 'possession of the field,' are historians to be replaced by 'numerous groups of aggressive and confident workers in the same field who ask not what was the fact . . . but . . . what is the ultimate explanation of history?'[18] Barzun is less apocalyptic in *Clio and the Doctors*. He understands the frustrations that drive 'strong historical minds to seek the laws of history'; they are seduced by a fantasy of sufficiency, and 'the product of this desire bears the name "philosophy of history."' 'No one would then question the utility of history, nor could withhold his attention from it. The ravishing Clio would need no doctors, but rather – like Penelope besieged by suitors – a bodyguard.' 'The sad contortions and false simplicities of all the philosophies of history so far written are enough,' he says, 'to disqualify them at the base' although, 'in spite of its irremediable defects the philosophy of history, like other aberrations of misplaced love, has not been without benefits.'[19] And yet despite this resistance to meta-textual concerns my historian suffers a certain unease about the narrative habits and practices he inherits from a long history of history as narrativizing. Since I have invented this figure, he is male, and thus representative both statistically and attitudinally – which is to say that he engages primarily the works of other male historians, and he sees as important those details and evidence typically seen as important among historians over time.

The working historian might very well lodge a protest against this generalizing procedure, despite historiography's own history of reproductions within the paradigms of 'great men' and 'heroes,' and all the more because he might argue that historians who choose to write books on historiography are no more representative of the earthier majority within the guild than those who imagine a 'philosophy of history.' But, while it may be suggested that historians who write about the doing of historiography select themselves because of a congenital predisposition toward philosophizing, this is a premise that, although it may be neither conclusively verified nor conclusively invalidated, overlooks certain mundane facts. The less existential assumption (and the one that follows Gay's advice about the rule of parsimony dictated in

---

[18] George Burton Adams, 'History and the Philosophy of History,' *American Historical Review*, 14, 2 (January 1909), 229–30.

[19] Barzun, *Clio and the Doctors*, 119–20.

Occam's razor) is that there is a connection between the generalized assertions of the first kind of discussion – on the idea of history – and the procedures within the second – historiography – and it is an assumption borne out by the fact that the men who write about the idea of history usually do so after long experience with the writing of history. Gay speaks of the time 'when historians settle down to reflect about their business – a self-conscious, not always felicitous venture into philosophical rumination they are often seduced to undertake after they have reached the age of fifty.'[20] And he makes this claim in the preface of his own book on historiography, a text that is doubly informed by his own experience as an historian and by his evaluations of the historians whose work and whose critical assessments of others' work have provided the context for his conclusions. Rather than distinguishing the philosopher-historians and the historians as two separate breeds, then, one could reasonably argue that the two modes are interdependent. It seems likely that the historian who writes about historiography is not more metaphysically inclined than his hands-on brothers, but that he is more open to the 'seduction,' as Gay calls it, of analyzing his dilemma as an historian. This conjecture is not contradictory to Gay's temporal theory, which would suggest that the capacity to be seduced into such analyses is developmentally determined.

It is the case, nonetheless, that the very question, 'What is history?' implies a philosophy of history or, as Gay calls it in *Freud for Historians*, an 'historical epistemology.'[21] The enterprise of arriving at an epistemology is most usually grounded in meta-physical assumptions and, if the historian is also philosophically trained like R. G. Collingwood, in standard metaphysical termi-nology; even if the enterprise is felt to fail, the defeat is signaled in language that presupposes the metaphysical field which provoked the effort. Gay goes on in his description of historians seduced into the realm of philosophy to say that these forays usually end up with the historians professing 'themselves pronounced subjectivists,' and subjectivism does indeed run throughout many of these reveries as evidence of the metaphysical duress under which they have practiced their craft of history-writing. But of course subjectivism is a theme that is predicated within standard

---

[20] Gay, *Freud for Historians*, 186; viii.   [21] *Ibid.*, viii.

metaphysical terms, since the opposite and never entirely lost ideal is 'objectivism' (the resolution would not be 'metaphysical' or 'not-metaphysical' but 'externally legitimated' or 'not externally legitimated'). The standard warning, articulated over and over, is that the historian walks through the Scylla of complete skepticism and the Charybdis of some externally imposed systematic, diametric oppositions that can only be conceived within the embrace of an overarching metaphysical structure. One must assume that this anxiety arises experientially, as the historian does his work, rather than from some independent or latter-day metaphysical bias.

It may be argued, then, that those historians who articulate this larger question, 'What is history/historiography?' tend only to articulate metaphysical assumptions that the working historian may more easily bracket for the space of his given enterprise. George Burton Adams' formula is telling in this regard, as it conflates the philosophical and theological: 'The field of the historian is, and must long remain, the discovery and recording of what actually happened . . . But this does not preclude his cherishing a philosophy of history . . . He may well hold to the belief that the facts which he is establishing tend to prove this or that final explanation of history. By such a belief his labors may be lightened and rendered more effective.'[22] While it is almost possible to imagine an historian so pragmatically and materialistically inclined as to be Edenically innocent of all post-positivist anxieties, one would have to place such a figure among the holy fools who remain untouched by the corruptions and sophistications that surround them. Yet, certainly, some historians are more unselfconscious than others, and one could go further and suggest that the historian who chooses to write about the idea of history – who attempts, however unsuccessful he feels the effort to have been, to ask 'What is history?' – will more fully *create* for himself the metaphysical anxieties that underlie his attempts to tell the historical truth. The very act of clearly articulating philosophical and methodological questions brings them into existence in a way that more nascent or repressed unease does not. But the difference is in measure, not in kind, since historians know too much history, and know too well their placedness within history to remain completely innocent of the larger interrogations surrounding their

---

[22] Adams, 'History and the Philosophy of History,' 236.

discourse. The historian who writes about historiography may reasonably be imagined, then, to have *yielded* to the need to confront what are in fact the more generalized anxieties within the guild regarding practice, while the others remain hard-working and stoically non-philosophical (with all of the contradictions implied in that last oxymoron). But, as with any crisis of faith, even the expression of doubt is a paradoxical affirmation of belief; the truly fallen do not turn to producing books on historiography but to novel-writing or to silence or to law school.

Conclusion

This undertaking will not attempt to offer any large-scale feminist correctives or any answers to the legitimation crisis that has sent shock waves through even the most recalcitrantly conservative historians.[23] But neither is it meant to argue for an indeterminacy which, because it cannot be breached, must halt historiography in its tracks: its aim is not apocalyptic, and it has no fear that the end of history has arrived. Although aggressive in its interrogations, it is also aware of the impossibility, anatomized by Lyotard in *The Differend*, of proving oneself the victim of an injustice that cannot be named or seen; in this case that injustice might be felt as an irresponsible impugning of historiography's internal consistency with no offer of reparation for damages. As victims learn through hard experience, 'It is impossible to establish one's innocence, in and of itself. It is a nothingness.'[24] As Lyotard says, 'The defense is nihilistic, the prosecution pleads for existents'; and in this case it might seem, as if, by offering no grand ameliorations in exchange for an attack on history's good name, I am taking the easy route of nihilism, stealing something ineffable and then waiting comfortably as the prosecution attempts to describe what it has lost.[25]

Yet, while the impulse is indeed a judicial one, the arguments here are meant to accomplish something very small: they would hope merely to stand as a warning that forgetfulness is far too

[23] See Jurgen Habermas, *The Legitimation Crisis*, and Jean François Lyotard's response in *The Postmodern Condition: A Report on Knowledge*, trans. Geoff Bennington and Brian Massumi (Minneapolis: University of Minnesota Press, 1988).

[24] Jean François Lyotard, *The Differend: Phrases in Dispute*, trans. Georges Van Den Abbeele (Minneapolis: University of Minnesota Press, 1988), 9.

[25] Lyotard, *The Differend*, 9.

easy, and that a forgetfulness carried out within the terms of tradition and in the language of the dominant discourse will tend to perpetuate amnesias and myths, Oedipal and otherwise, about certain traditionally unimportant and unseen groups of people. And if the people are forgotten so too is a world of thought, language, and experience that may very well have little to do with accepted wisdoms about 'man' and may very well have surprising new perspectives to offer. It seems to me that the only safeguard to writing narratively about history (or anything else that pretends toward truth) is a thoroughly shaken complacency. Like Frost's speaker in 'Mending Wall,' I am not entirely disinclined to pick a fight, but, like him, 'Before I built a wall I'd ask to know / What I was walling in or walling out, / And to whom I was like to give offense.' This does not prevent him from giving offense, or a fence, but it does suggest that he knows himself to be implicated in the irony of the situation. I would only wish, then, to keep the questions alive about how one writes in any discipline that claims that its obligation is to look for truth in a non-fictional, non-poetic way; for to enact a purpose, to tell a felt truth, to persuade, to recreate, to re-enact the past, to undertake any of those necessary and often commendable gestures of putting words out into the world necessitates selectivity and exclusion.

One cannot *do* everything, nor should one be under the obligation to try, but a fully activated memory of contextual issues should extend beyond the pursuit of a traditionally defined 'historical' context to include the concentricities in which thought and action occur. There is no logical necessity that these interrogations will end in paralysis and dark skepticism, or that they will force the historian into writing like a theoretician, divesting him of that crucial identificatory mark, his own style.[26] To accuse and berate recent theoretically informed or feminist historiography, as G. R. Elton does in his 1990 Cook Lectures, is to close off the very contextual impulse to which he so bitterly fears theory will 'prove fatal' (and one should not, I think, take the intemperance of Elton's comments as marginal within the discourse, since they are sanctioned by the authority of the Cook Lectures at the University of Michigan and published under the considerable academic authority of Cambridge University Press). To attack the 'theory-

---

[26] See Peter Gay, *Style in History*, (New York: Basic Books, 1974), especially 3–17.

mongers' is easy enough, particularly when the assault is undertaken with the messianic sense that one is 'fighting for the lives of innocent young people beset by devilish tempters who claim to offer higher forms of thought and deeper truths and insights – the intellectual equivalent of crack, in fact.'[27] This is a perennial theme, and a dangerous one in itself. One sees another version of it in Conyers Read's controversial 1950 presidential address to the American Historical Society, 'The Social Responsibility of the Historian.' Here, with the advantage of hindsight, one sees that the extremisms it unknowingly licenses are soon to be fully embodied in McCarthyism: 'If historians, in their examination of the past, represent the evolution of civilization as haphazard, without direction and without progress, offering no assurance that mankind's present position is on the highway and not on some dead end, then mankind will seek for assurance in a more positive alternative whether it be offered from Rome or Moscow . . . This sounds like the advocacy of one form of social control as against another. In short, it is . . . Not everything that takes place in the laboratory is appropriate for broadcast at the streetcorners.'[28]

Read may advocate what is felt by others to be an objectionable or dangerous censoring, but in speaking with complete candor he offers the possibility of open debate: his argument *performs* and sustains the very freedom that it questions. But more covert programs of censorship, enacted by capitalizing on Oedipal paranoia, betray the very spirit of history-writing itself. Anti-theoretical, anti-philosophical, and anti-feminist, they promote a narrowly hegemonic vision of what counts as worth remembering and thinking about by discounting all the rest as unmanly. One who allows himself, as does Elton, to speak in a public lecture of 'the cancerous radiation that comes from the forehead of Derrida and Foucault' with the parenthetical joke appended, '(stop that metaphor),' cannot be applauded for openmindedness, yet the Rush Limbaugh tactics are undeniably powerful, and at a level less susceptible to analysis or conversation.[29] In the space of a few pages, Elton dismisses Heidegger, Adorno, Saussure, Barthes, Derrida, Foucault, and Gadamer, not to mention a long list of

[27] Elton, *Return to Essentials* (Cambridge University Press, 1991), 41.
[28] Conyers Read, 'The Social Responsibility of the Historian,' *American Historical Review*, 55, 2 (January 1950), 284. See, too, Howard K. Beale, 'The Professional Historian,' 254.   [29] Elton, *Return to Essentials*, 41.

historians, including Hayden White and the 'fanatical feminist,' Joan Wallach Scott.[30] One does not have to agree with Collingwood that all history is the re-enactment of past thought to believe that thinking, past and present, is a crucial enough activity that it does not bear circumscription; one does not have to be among the Faustian damned to imagine that the crucial activity of historical reconstruction requires as capacious a set of cerebral possibilities as it is possible to get. One does not have to be an historian to understand the importance, the power, and the necessity of historiography. And one does not have to step through the looking-glass to have the sense of being in a world where one has to run very fast just to stay still.

Memory, memoirs, remembrance: historiography always has a vested concern in this issue of memory. Its apprehension of the concept, 'memory,' is not likely to be simple, for any theory of memory will call forth certain alleged distinctions that must be recognized: one who must evaluate sources has to attempt to discriminate among the relatively 'simple' and unencumbered (and therefore potentially reliable) memory of a past event, the more complex Proustian memory, which is not dependably recallable because involuntary but which may, when it comes, be felt as profoundly reliable, and the 'memory' which is more felt and performed than consciously acknowledged. As Collingwood puts it, 'To go about short of a leg is not the same thing as remembering the loss of it, and to suffer a neurotic disability as the result of fear is not the same thing as remembering the fear.'[31] There are all kinds of tricks in memory's bag, and this the historian well knows. Yet he deals in memory nonetheless. Carl Becker writes, 'The chief value of history is that it is an extension of the personal memory, and an extension which masses of people can share, so that it becomes, or would ideally become, the memory of a nation, or of humanity. In so far as it does or can do this it should serve to steady the activities and fortify and fructify the purposes of mankind.'[32] To bring a past, in something like the fullness of its power or its horror, into the present in such a way as to force it to

[30] *Ibid.*, 27–40.
[31] Collingwood, 'Some Perplexities Concerning Time,' *Proceedings of the Aristotelian Society*, vol. 26 (1925–26), 144.
[32] Michael Kammen, ed. *'What is the Good of History?': Selected Letters of Carl L. Becker, 1900–1945* (Ithaca: Cornell University Press, 1973), 86.

some restitution by making the people who read about it more thoughtful and less complacent: this is one of the classic tasks of History. To memorialize so sufficiently as to effect some always limited, always partial recuperation in the present, to make people *remember* what they do not know first-hand and to recognize in what they do know the dangers of the past that are alive in the present: this is one of the classic tasks of History. One need not take whole-cloth Collingwood's re-enactment theory of history to recognize that good historiography has a performative force, bringing the past into the present, not just for the hell of it, but to make a difference in the present. The worlds it makes perform at some level the task of making the world we are in. Forgetfulness is necessary to construct any narrative of any kind because so much must be left out to speak a story in words arranged syntactically; but narrative-writing itself *produces* forgetfulness as well, and it can lull its teller into a sense of completeness as it carries him along within a telos whose energies are to some large extent self-contained. This does not mean that historians should stop writing narrative and start writing 'theory,' but is only to suggest that all the rich variations within the historiographic enterprise be undertaken with a full sense of the difficulties of the task. So my efforts here are modest and they are undertaken with the intuition that there is nothing for it but to do one's work as a fully conscious pragmatist, or, alternatively, as a poet.

1

Oedipal pedagogy: becoming a woman

It is my opinion that Professor Flechsig must have had some idea of this tendency, innate in the Order of the World, whereby in certain conditions the unmanning of a human being is provided for; perhaps he thought of this himself or these ideas were inspired in him by divine rays, which I think is more likely. A *fundamental misunderstanding* obtained however, which has since run like a red thread through my entire life. It is based upon the fact *that, within the Order of the World, God did not really understand the living human being* and had no need to understand him, because, according to the Order of the World, He dealt only with corpses.

Daniel Paul Schreber, Memoirs of My Nervous Illness

> Jesse Belle: Can you interpret dreams? I dreamed last night
> Someone took curved nail-scissors and snipped off
> My eyelids so I couldn't shut my eyes
> To anything that happened anymore.
>
> Robert Frost, 'A Masque of Mercy'

Oedipal bodies

In psychohistory, if they are not consigned to oblivion, if they are evidentially present enough to demand the researcher's attention, women inevitably emerge in the only way the Oedipal story will let them be seen: as the sources of problems, the reasons for failures, as the artifact from the past that has compromised the son in the present. And if they are not present, and they so often are not because they have not documented themselves in conventional ways, and if, in an Oedipal catch-22 that renders them invisible, they have not been recovered historiographically, they are either sentimentalized or felt more explicitly as insufficient, their absence (from the text, from texts) evidence of a failure to intervene in the bullying or overcompensational mothering suffered under the father's hand. Because the psychohistorical literature is the (disguised) fulfillment of a (repressed) wish to confront the

Father/God within whose unendurable, necessary, causative presence the circumstantialities that make up history might safely unfold, this sacrificial rite becomes somewhat less covert than in standard histories. In psychohistory the gloves come off, and historiography's oedipalized/feminized relationship with metaphysics reveals itself in the only fully authorized version allowable: in the heterosexually but homophilically vigorous, semiotically enriched, historically licensed misogyny of the Oedipus fantasy (the specific deployment in psychohistory of the Freudian Oedipus Complex is, as I have said, merely a more formal enactment of a generalized initiating narrative). Proof of the good son, the psychohistoriographic sacrifice of the mother reifies the mode by which conventional historiography must proceed; perhaps it is this direct embodiment into the unendurable specifics of the Oedipus Complex fantasy, this virtual allegorization of a more clandestine or repressed historiographic process, that makes historians generally so antipathetic to the genre.

In fact, as a correlative issue, one could assert that the two genres share very fluid boundaries, so much so that categorizations often seem willful or only retroactively pertinent. Because one of the tenets of psychohistory and psychobiography is that technical language be retranslated into more accessible terms, it is often very hard to decide whether a text is working from an explicitly psychoanalytic point of view or whether psychoanalytically inclined readers impose this framework on a text whose terms are congenial to, but not generated by, that discourse. It is also the case, as for instance in E. R. Dodds' *The Greeks and the Irrational*, that a very occasional reference to Freud or some other psychoanalytic authority may or may not be used by evaluators to locate the text within psychohistory, simply because the extent of influence is not at all clear.

Psychohistory exposes historiography's secrets (which is why historians tend to take the matter so personally), not because it is methodologically more rigorous or because it is privy to human 'truth.' The exposure is not at the constative but at the performative level (the 'do as I say, not as I do' distinction), for psychohistory enacts the identificatory process by which 'History' is claimed as 'real,' as evidentially true, and as 'objective' from within a domain felt as material and contiguous; enacting a vivid and immediate dramatization of historiography's own internal conflicts, the psychohistoriographic players come into a larger play in progress, like the wandering troupe in *Hamlet* who stage the hidden terms of paternal murder in lurid detail for all the court to see. Psychohistory performs the historiographer's intimate relationship with his subject, History – the subject, after all, of 'great men' – as metonymous, and as transferentially complex rather than as objectively analytical, even as it lays claim through psychoanalytic theory to a set of clinically verifiable truths.

The psychobiographer's intense relationship with his (usually male) subject will almost necessarily produce an identification which, even if fraught with ambivalence, will pull the observer more inevitably into the gravity of the semiotically dense Oedipal fantasy; these studies enact through the paradox of transference history's conflictual and profoundly enriched relationship to metaphysics, and the ontotheological bias by which Truth/God/ Father erects itself in the enduring fantasy of Great Men, i.e. those virilely moderate, non-excessive, externally directed creatures whose virtues reveal themselves by performing antitheses to 'femaleness.'[1] One need only read a few psychobiographies to see this a priori dismissal, sentimental or pejorative, of the female. The Georges' biography of Woodrow Wilson contains a representative formulation of the sentimental type:

Wilson's mother was a rather plain, serious woman, extremely reserved, greatly devoted to her family. There is little in the historical record on the boy's relationship with his mother . . . 'I remember how I clung to her (a laughed-at-'mama's boy') till I was a great big fellow,' Wilson wrote of his mother many years later in a letter to his wife. 'But love of the best womanhood came to me and entered my heart through those apronstrings. If I had not lived with such a mother I could not have won and seemed to deserve – in part, perhaps, deserved, through transmitted virtues – such a wife.'[2]

Apparently benign, superficially conscientious, this kind of formulation almost masks a killing indifference; presumably a major player in this Oedipal drama, the mother is blithely lost to history, the fact that 'there is little in the historical record on the boy's relationship with his mother' apparently a matter of only very

[1] See Dominick LaCapra, 'History and Psychoanalysis,' in *The Trials of Psychoanalysis*, ed. Francoise Meltzer (University of Chicago Press, 1988), 14–16.
[2] Alexander L. George and Juliette George, *Woodrow Wilson and Colonel House: A Personality Study* (New York: Dover, 1964), 5–6.

small concern, historically and psychoanalytically speaking. For, after all, the choice of Wilson's letter to his wife tells all one needs to know about the Oedipal situation, and it does the double duty, as is so often the case, of pretending homage while adding insult to injury ('a laughed-at mama's boy,' 'apron strings,' etc.). This, I would venture, is not done consciously, but happens merely as the result of those textual, methodological, and symbolic habits that stitch history out of men and allegories out of women.

On the one hand taboo, and on the other already known in the ahistorical substance of femaleness, 'mother' marks a place that is felt to transcend the less-than-human female breeders whose specific traces in time are irrelevant; as the above letter conflating mother and wife makes clear, this equation takes care of all kinds of business at once, establishing a single empty denseness in which typological 'woman' rests. It should be noted that such absences cannot, under Oedipal rules, make the heart grow fonder since, as the father rises up into monstrosity – as, for example, he does in the Schreber corpus or as he does for the Georges' Wilson – the mother's implied failure to intervene becomes either explicitly or implicitly culpable. Maynard Solomon's *Beethoven*, with its double process of innuendo and more active discrediting relative to the mother, is paradigmatic and has disturbing echoes in recent revelations about judicial, reportorial, and political repressions of the facts of domestic violence: 'It is nowhere recorded that Maria Magdalena protested her husband's treatment of her eldest son,' Solomon writes, and thus she is implicated irrevocably in domestic tyrant Johann's abuse of the child; the neighbors reported 'that the mother's care in externals was not always of the best' (ah, she must have been depressed, hypochondriacal, typically neurotic); Gottfried Fischer asserted that 'the Beethoven children were not delicately brought up; they were often left with the maids' (ah, she was irresponsible, and where did she go, after all, when she left her children?); Cäcilia Fischer confirmed that Beethoven was 'often dirty and negligent.'[3] Solomon concludes his paragraph on Beethoven's mother with the standard theme: 'As we will see in a later chapter, Beethoven's difficulties in establishing a love relationship with a woman, as well as his tendencies toward misogyny, may have had their

[3] Maynard Solomon, *Beethoven* (New York: Schirmer Books, 1977), 18.

26

origin in his unsatisfying relationship with his mother.'[4] In this context of implicature, it is interesting to read Heinz Kohut's analysis of Pauline Haas Schreber: Schreber's 'mother was subordinated to, submerged by, and interwoven with the father's overwhelming personality and strivings, thus permitting the son no refuge from the impact of the father's pathology.'[5]

And, if the father rises up humanized, then he is accorded a maternal as well as a paternal sufficiency that suggests his filling of a need created by the mother's lack; and in any case, whether or not the historical mother in historical fact adopted a policy of non-intervention, her absence from the text will guarantee that she is so perceived. This forgetfulness spreads like a virus from text to text, from mother to wife to daughter: in her 1994 review of Svi Lothane's *In Defense of Schreber: Soul Murder and Psychiatry*, Rosemary Dinnage writes:

Too little is known also about Schreber's wife, Sabine . . . The couple's adopted daughter, Fridoline, told an interviewer in her old age that her adoptive father was 'more of a mother to me than my mother'; she preferred him, because he was 'loving, just and kind.' There is some mystery about Fridoline's adoption and it has even been suggested that she was Sabine's illegitimate daughter, but there is no proof.[6]

Implicature is a powerful thing, and Sabine, undocumented black hole as she is, draws suspicion down upon herself.

So Sabine was – well, you know – and Frau Beethoven was a sloven, but either side of this coin would be equally defaced; one can look at Freud's reading of Dora's mother as suffering from housewife syndrome to see how a more rigorous hygenics might have been read.

From the accounts given me by the girl and her father I was led to imagine her as an uncultivated woman and above all as a foolish one, who had concentrated all her interests on domestic affairs, especially since her husband's illness and the estrangement to which it led. She presented the picture, in fact, of what might be called the 'housewife's psychosis.' She had no understanding for her children's more active interests, and was occupied all day long in cleaning the house with its furniture and utensils

[4] *Ibid.*, 18.
[5] Quoted in Han Israels, *Schreber: Father and Son*, trans. H. S. Lake (Madison, Ct.: Internation University Press, Inc., 1989), 92.
[6] Rosemary Dinnage, review of *In Defense of Schreber*, *New York Review of Books*, March 3, 1994, 19.

and in keeping them clean – to such an extent as to make it almost impossible to use or enjoy them.'[7]

And this woman, too, marks a place where analysis need not go: 'This condition,' Freud continues, 'traces of which are to be found often enough in normal housewives, inevitably reminds one of forms of obsessional washing and other kinds of obsessional cleanliness. But such women (and this applied to the patient's mother) are entirely without insight into their illness, so that one essential characteristic of an 'obsessional neurosis' is lacking.'[8] Damned if you do, damned if you don't, since it all boils down in the end to the necessities of the Oedipal story.

Thomas Kohut's whole-cloth investment in his father's self-psychology produces a particularly virulent strain of Oedipalizing in *Wilhelm II and the Germans*, with chapter headings on the mother entitled, 'The Legacy of Maternal Worry and Disappointment,' 'The Legacy of Maternal Possessiveness.' Victoria is predisposed to 'fault-finding,' and 'obsessive worry'; Wilhelm is burdened by her 'oppressive sense of irresponsibility.' The standard pathologizing of the mother in Kohut's text seems particularly willful given the immense political, social, familial, dynastic, military, and physiological complexities of the case; but, in addition to a sense that the Oedipal triad of bad mother, weak father, and damaged son is more than ordinarily Procrustean here, one who reads in Kohut's text written documents from Victoria herself will find that they make a far from unambiguous statement regarding her maternal sufficiency. His interpretations of them are, to my eyes, oddly skewed; and if we are all blind men around an elephant in the matter of interpretation it nonetheless seems that he has grabbed a particularly tiny piece. In other words, it is as if Kohut's own Oedipal blindness – and one cannot help but wonder about his unqualified appropriation of Kohutian psychology, while at the same time mentioning his father directly only in the notes – dictates a reduction of Victoria before the fact that is so compelling that it subsumes the complexities of her mothering into a unilateral reading. (One might almost apply father Kohut's reading of Pauline Schreber, 'subordinated to, submerged by, and interwoven with the father's overwhelming personality and striv-

---

[7] Sigmund Freud, *Dora: An Analysis of a Case of Hysteria* (New York: Collier, 1963), 34–35.   [8] *Ibid.*, 35.

ings.') Yet, in this negative assessment of Victoria, Kohut affiliates himself as well with Father Freud, who says regarding Wilhelm's case: 'It is usual for mothers whom Fate has presented with a child who is sickly or otherwise at a disadvantage to try to compensate him for his unfair handicap by a superabundance of love. In the instance before us, the proud mother behaved otherwise; she withdrew her love from the child on account of his infirmity. When he had grown up into a man of great power, he proved unambiguously by his actions that he had never forgiven his mother. When you consider the importance of a mother's love for the mental life of a child, you will no doubt make a tacit correction of the biographer's inferiority theory.'[9]

Polite innuendo and not so polite aggression run forward with the full inertial momentum of history, but even good intentions pave the same road to hell as long as they yield to the decorums of conventional historiography's reticence about women. Han Israels, had he been less chronically ambivalent, could have done much more with his sense, in *Schreber: Father and Son*, that certain controlling narratives – the wife as 'will-less victim of her husband,' the 'domestic tyrant' story – shape expectations about females to an insidious degree. Svi Lothane attempts to recover Pauline Schreber as 'a matriarch of towering strength,' despite the fact that 'in the few sources that have come down to us, the emphasis is on the father and little about the mother.' 'I suspect that the love between mother and son was at least as important in Schreber's character formation as was his love for his father,' says Lothane, but because of the vast discrepancies in documentation and the inertial force of misogyny, this suspicion of maternal sufficiency can only be heard faintly or filtered through the sentimentalized code one sees in Wilson's letter to his wife. Lacking as it does all historically dense detailing, and lacking, too, a historical context in which women, through such detailing and specificity, might emerge from caricature and fantasy, this well-intended gesture falls short.[10] Assertions of female and maternal sufficiency must be made by sheer force of will within a field of discourse in which the father prevails.

---

[9] Sigmund Freud, *New Introductory Lectures on Psychoanalysis*, trans. James Strachey (New York: W. W. Norton & Co. 1965), 59.

[10] Svi Lothane, *In Defense of Schreber: Soul Murder and Psychiatry* (Hillsdale, N.J.: The Analytic Press, 1992), 16, 443.

One who reads from a feminist perspective is left profoundly uneasy in all of this, for it becomes clear that under Oedipal law there is no such thing as a fair trial for the mother. Robert Frost's morality play, 'A Masque of Reason,' lets Job's wife articulate this paradox just before she nods off to sleep and the men get on to the more important matter of Job's education into God's ways: 'God's had / Aeons of time and still it's mostly women / Get burned for prophecy, men almost never,' she says. And indeed, John Demos' study of witchcraft, *Entertaining Satan*, confirms Mrs. Job's complaint, even as it unselfconsciously participates in the Oedipal system that helped produce the trials. Demos' highly detailed reading of the case of Elizabeth Knapp calls upon Freudian theories of hysteria and other psychoanalytic devices, and then makes a move that seems nearly inevitable to psychobiographical assessment:

As to her mother, there is no hard information; but a fragment from a contemporaneous diary suggests important – and highly plausible – possibilities. The source is the Boston merchant John Hull, the time 'about 1658,' the substance as follows.

There was a woman of [illeg.], Knapp; pretending to rail, and being troublesome, she was sent to prison. Sometimes she would hate Quakers, sometimes plead for them; sometimes weeping tears, she could, out of herself, speak not a word to any; sometimes weary others with much speaking.

Was this Elizabeth [Warren] Knapp? The absence, in Hull's notation, of a given name forbids certainty. Perhaps, then, this family drama presented not only an adulterous father but also a seriously disturbed mother. (And perhaps the *two* developments were interconnected).[11]

My point is not that Demos is necessarily unjustified in making these connections, but only that the same Oedipal habits that predispose him to be relatively disinterested in making a sustained analysis of the larger, acutely significant, and statistically meaningful phenomenon of gender bias in witchcraft accusations will predispose him to make this standard leap. One of the commonest formulations in psychohistory and psychobiography is, 'As to the mother, there is no hard information; but . . . '

[11] John Putnam Demos, *Entertaining Satan: Witchcraft and the Culture of Early New England* (New York: Oxford University Press, 1983), 112.

If, as Freud says, Wilhelm 'proved unambiguously by his actions that he had never forgiven his mother,' one can only shrug, for with the Oedipal story as prime directive this grudge will always enjoy either covert or overt sanction. Whatever Beethoven's mother, or Wilhelm's mother, or Picasso's mother might actually have been like, and whatever these women might or might not have done relative to their families (and I do not pretend to offer an alternative history), the evidence will be selected before the fact to fit the Oedipal case and deployed and analyzed in predetermined ways. This reaction is multiply overdetermined: one cannot, for example, forget that a historiography dependent on documentation will find itself, even when it troubles to look elsewhere, with far more material, both primary and secondary, about and by men than about and by women. It is fruitless to speculate about the cause and effect of this fact; the mere fact of an absence will perpetuate a narrative of absence or insufficiency or passivity. And, in the usual double bind, those women who manage to intrude themselves upon history will, by virtue of having done it, risk being assigned to the opposite pole of a presence that is untoward, a sufficiency that is whorish or excessive, and an agressivity to be deplored. Passed by the brotherhood down through time and language, the Oedipal myth becomes so deeply infused that it emerges with articulation itself, and the tautologies within which misogyny is sustained are thus invisible.

Yet psychobiography only allegorizes, using the figures of Father and Son, a more generally institutionalized, more successful repression within psychohistoriography and within conventional historiography, whose covert negotiation of the Oedipal contract is marked from the start by indifference to and amnesia about mother-figures and women. *History*, as Hegel baldly asserts, occurs only when the intimate affiliations of the family unit yield to a larger order; the Antigones are vital to this process, for resistance to their personalized versions of justice and responsibility is the proof of a more manly and selfless commitment to the larger scheme. (Sophocles, with his uncanny instinct for the definitive, does it again in the sequel: Antigone, buried alive as if to predict history's necessary effacement of the 'female,' the cautionary absence who, unearthed, will always upset the Oedipal applecart.) Whether historiography's oedipalized narratives justify a predisposition toward misogyny or exacerbate it, or both, is unclear; that there is a history of such dismissiveness is an indisputable commonplace. At the most obvious level, there is a convenient forgetfulness regarding women that is reflected in endless negotiations within a formula whereby history is up for grabs as either 'the biography of great men,' Carlyle's position, or as 'the science of men in time,' Bloch's formulation. One hardly needs to say that it would be unpardonable sophistry in the context of its specific preoccupations to argue that historiography's long history of speaking of 'men' and 'man' and 'Western man' and 'mankind' has signaled an equal and inclusive interest in women through a 'universal' designation; at best traditional historiographers have thought of woman as she is married to man, and they have implicitly endorsed the Victorian formulation which says to the wife, 'We are one, and I am he.' (Or as Blackstone's *Commentaries* says, 'Husband and wife are one person in the law; that is, the very being or legal existence of the woman is suspended during marriage.') As with guilds in general, this one has not in the past been welcoming to or particularly interested in women.

One could take as emblematic the complex series of moves that opens the Vintage Books edition of Marc Bloch's *The Historian's Craft*, for it is a most elegant and moving display of Oedipal energies in which the mother/wife is a deferred presence within an interchange among men. Introduced by Joseph Strayer and translated by Peter Putnam, it opens with four successive documents that prepare one for Bloch's own opening gambit in the text proper: '"Tell me, Daddy. What is the use of history?" Thus, a few years ago, a young lad in whom I had a very special interest questioned his historian father.'[12] These words are preceded by a complex set of negotiations among men, a precedent Bloch himself had set in *Rois et serfs*, which contains a dedication proper, to his father Gustav ('à mon père, son élève'), and in the acknowledgments an embedded dedication to his mentor Christian Pfister (a name 'that would have been inscribed at the opening of these pages if . . . I had not felt I should dedicate my thesis to another of my masters who has been teaching me for an even longer time').[13]

[12] Marc Bloch, *The Historian's Craft*, trans. Peter Putnam (New York: Vintage Books, 1953), 3.
[13] Natalie Davis, 'History's Two Bodies,' *American Historical Review*, 93, 1 (February 1988), 22–23.

The document that opens the text is prominently titled 'To Lucien Febvre, By Way of a Dedication,' and it begins:

If this book should one day be published – if, begun as a simple antidote by which, amid sorrows and anxieties both personal and collective, I seek a little peace of mind, it should turn into a real book, intended to be read – you will find, my friend, another name than yours inscribed upon its dedication page. You can surmise the name this place requires; it is the one permissible allusion to a tenderness too deep and sacred to be spoken. Yet how can I resign myself to seeing you appear in no more than a few chance references? Long have we worked together for a wider and more human history . . . But the time will come, I feel sure, when our collaboration can again be public, and again be free. Meanwhile, it is in these pages filled with your presence that, for my part, our joint work goes on.

The first thing among the many that could be said about this classic statement of friendship is that nowhere within the front matter of *The Historian's Craft* is there another name than Febvre's inscribed openly upon a dedication page; the second is that Bloch's internal reference to 'the name this place requires' seems almost palimpsestic, a covering of wife over mother or vice versa. Febvre's own similarly embedded reference to Bloch's wife – 'as a matter of dedication and of solemn memory' – within his editorial introduction implies that Bloch's elliptical notation is meant to suggest Simone Vidal Bloch, 'Madame Marc Bloch.' But when Bloch writes, 'You can surmise the name this place requires; it is the one permissible allusion to a tenderness too deep and sacred to be spoken,' one knows only a nameless synonymity. Bloch might better have written 'the place this name requires': the place 'woman/mother/wife.'

There is nothing egregiously wrong here, nothing noticeable really, or worth mentioning, really, except how naturally and how quietly the lacuna resides, an irremediable absence that is not at all felt as an absence. *The Historian's Craft* was, of course, published posthumously from a manuscript that Febvre claims to have reproduced scrupulously and one that at Bloch's death was not at the final pre-publication stage at which the dedication page is written out. Yet there is sufficient documentary evidence to allow Natalie Davis, in 'History's Two Bodies,' to write: 'Bloch planned a characteristic double dedication to *Métier d'historien*: it was to be dedicated to the memory of his late mother, and the letter to Febvre was to be included 'by way of dedication.'' There is a letter from Bloch to his son, Etienne, written September 13, 1942, several months before Bloch joined the Resistance, discussing the title: 'Afternoons I'm working especially on my book (*Historian's Craft* seems to me a better title than *Apology for History*. What do you think?)'[14] There is a complex history to this history and to the history of Bloch's dedicatory habits, but it emerges as a story among men, Gustav Bloch, Etienne Bloch, Lucien Febvre, Marc Bloch, Christian Pfister.

But Bloch's address to Febvre is irresistible, a model expression of filial love, within a long history of such expressions; it would be redundant to speak here of 'male' friendship, since the discourse of friendship is canonical, and it presumes the impossibility of there being any other kind. As Derrida says in 'The Politics of Friendship,' 'a *double exclusion* . . . can be seen at work in all the great ethico-politico-philosophical discourses on friendship, namely on the one hand the exclusion of friendship between women, and, on the other hand, the exclusion of friendship between a man and a woman.'[15] The play is among men, with the phantom of this unnamed woman in the far background, and the stakes are nothing less than resurrection. Following Bloch's memorializing of Lucien Febvre is an introduction by Strayer that tells Bloch's own heroic story: a member of the Resistance, he was captured by the Germans in 1944, 'imprisoned, and cruelly mistreated. On June 16, as the Nazi hold on France began to weaken, he was taken from his cell and shot in an open field near Lyons with twenty-six other patriots' (viii-ix). After Strayer's introduction, Febvre himself speaks, in 'A Note on the Manuscripts of the Present Book.' He documents Bloch's intentions, gives a chronology, and attests to the scrupulous reproduction of the manuscript exactly as Bloch had left it: 'No addition, no correction, even of mere form has been supplied to Bloch's text; it is this text, pure and entire, which is to be found printed in this book' (xvii). One feels in Febvre's intent to reproduce Bloch's manuscript 'pure and entire' a powerful conflation of the body of the text and the body of the man himself. As it is brought to life, so too will Bloch be returned to the living.

---

[14] *Ibid.*, 23, 27–28.
[15] Jacques Derrida, 'The Politics of Friendship,' *The Philosophical Forum*, 85, p. 642. For a precise rendering of these assumptions within the fictional realm see, for example, D. H. Lawrence's *Women in Love*.

One finds this fantasy of the fully animated, living text articulated more explicitly elsewhere in genres such as lyric poetry; in fact, Shakespeare's sonnet 55 speaks directly to Febvre's conservation efforts, as it claims its fragile self – words on a page – as an antidote to history's worst foe, 'sluttish time,' which eradicates even memorials carved in stone. The loved friend will be animated, eternally erect and on the move: 'When wasteful war shall statues overturn, / And broils root out the work of masonry, / Nor Mars his sword nor war's quick fire shall burn / The living record of your memory. / Gainst death and all-oblivious enmity shall you pace forth.' Febvre's loving gesture is in a very real sense an attempt to embody his lost friend within his words (we will see another version of this gesture in Freud's reaction to Schreber's text); it is an exordium for a history whose function as last monument must come up against its performative effect as a text necessarily and most poignantly impromptu, unfinished, and informal. It is, as Barthes points out, always a difficult moment when historical discourse is inaugurated; the moment 'where we find in conjunction the beginning of the matter of the utterance and the *exordium* of the uttering' is, says Barthes, 'a solemn act of foundation.'[16] This elaborate preamble is a way to enfold Bloch, intact and individualized, within history, within the terms of his craft, and in relation to his brother historians; the prefatory matter, placed against Bloch's opening words, 'Tell me, Daddy. What is the use of history?' answers his question before the fact. These nested histories are a way to rebuke this latest inevitable cataclysm of violence by bringing back the dead. They are a way to exact restitution from a war that made Bloch say to him, 'We are vanquished, for a moment, by an unjust destiny.' Febvre intuits the paradox of infinite extension represented in these inked-in words against paper that can so easily crumble and burn. They *must* be endlessly reproduced, entered into history's book to be passed down. And as long as there are sons to say, 'Tell me, Daddy,' the lineage will extend itself unbroken through time.

The book *The Historian's Craft* that one holds in one's hands – the dedication, the introduction, the editor's comments, the translator's statement, is a memorial to a brother who has died. In order that this discourse of friendship be kept intact, in order that

[16] Roland Barthes, 'The Discourse of History,' trans. Stephen Bann, in *Comparative Criticism: A Yearbook*, ed. E. S. Shaffer (Cambridge University Press, 1981), 9.

Bloch's corpus be inscribed to its fullest extent in its proper place among men, Bloch's own promise must be broken: 'you will find, my friend, another name than yours inscribed upon its dedication page. You can surmise the name this place requires; it is the one permissible allusion to a tenderness too deep and sacred to be spoken.' Febvre ends his textual comments regarding Bloch's manuscript with this appended paragraph:

Finally, and because it is a matter both of dedication and of solemn memory, I cannot but say this:

There was a person to whom Marc Bloch, before departing, would have dedicated one of the great works we still expected from him. Those of us who knew and loved Marc Bloch were aware of the single-hearted tenderness with which she enveloped him and his children – and of that abnegation with which she had served him as secretary and helped in his labors. I feel it as an obligation which nothing can prevent me from meeting – not even that sense of sentimental reserve which was so strong with Marc Bloch – I feel it as a duty to set down here the name of Madame Marc Bloch, who died in the same cause as her husband and in the same French faith. (xviii)

There are some fairly poignant ironies in this apparently generous gesture, not the least of which is Febvre's pious assertion that Bloch, had he been given the opportunity, would have 'dedicated one of the great works that we still expected from him' to his wife. Not 'one of the great works we still expected from him,' one could say, but *this* only work, this last possible work, to this woman who has also died (how? – 'in the same cause . . . in the same French faith'). 'Because it is a matter both of dedication and of solemn memory, I cannot but say this . . . ': effectively cocooned within a textual arrangement which begins with 'To Lucien Febvre, by way of dedication,' the Madames Bloch appear as veiled necessity.

One does not have to be neurasthenic to feel the ironies that permeate this entire opening discourse, which ends with a brief translator's note in which Peter Putnam thanks his 'friend and teacher Robert R. Palmer, and [his] wife, Durinda.' Sentimentality, which places women obliquely within the historical picture as undifferentiated types (mother, secretary, wife), does at least acknowledge an existence in the background. But the double bind rules the discourse: if respectable, then unnamed, if not respectable (i.e. if particularly noticeable out in the world, where 'history' is made) then unworthy of consideration except perhaps as type.

Oedipal pedagogy: becoming a woman

This willed aporia is a dead giveaway to the oedipalized nature of historiography, proving the Oedipal lesson to have been taken to heart, for one *cannot* speak of the mother-figure directly but only through the obliquities of more socialized and acceptable desires. And where is one who is never given a full and proper name to be placed within history? Peter Gay talks, in *Style in History*, about the ways in which the historian's language and thinking are influenced by names from the past, and he himself makes a move so dense with the analogs that may be embedded within proper names that his statement stands as offering its truth at the level of assertion and of construction: Gay writes, 'Gibbon's Tacitean remark, "Augustus was sensible that mankind is governed by names," reads like a delicate acknowledgment of his debt.'[17] 'Mankind is governed by names,' says Augustus, says Tacitus, says Gibbon, says Gay, and the writing of history is inextricably bound within a system of historically named men and the historians who have named them. Madame Marc Bloch, 'who died in the same cause as her husband and in the same French faith,' is buried nameless within the very system that claims to see her as its dedicatory subject (it is interesting to note that Madame Bloch's death is treated as an extension of her husband's heroism, although she was not, like Bloch, executed, but died of cancer). And so, when Bloch begins, 'Tell me, Daddy. What is the use of history?' we know with all the force of subliminal suggestion that the question is to be answered among men and passed down through men.

And yet this forgetfulness of female existence as all but metaphor and allegory (Clio, that endangered virgin, stands aloof, while Madame Marc Bloch is the angel in the house) is only the tip of the iceberg. For a system that sets up any one of the metaphysical terms – God, Universal, Ideal, Center, Absolute, Presence, Substance – fully activates a spring-loaded linguistic system which, as it locates femaleness as the personification for all the terms antithetical to these absolutes, guarantees a reproduction of the standard devaluations. As David Musselwhite says in *Partings Welded Together*, 'language is machinic . . . "Feminine", "masculine", "housewife", "worker", "unemployed", "father" – these are not designations only, but *effects*: they bear upon deportment,

---

[17] Peter Gay, *Style in History* (New York: Basic Books, 1974), 30.

37

upon musculature, upon conduct. Language constitutes "senten-
ces" in the strongest sense of that term: we are "sentenced" to
being "male" or "female", "father" or "child" – even "alive" or
"dead."'[18] This system yields patterns of infinite deferment
(wonderfully illustrated in Ellman's *Thinking About Women*),
whereby terms shift incrementally to fit the a priori assumption of
a male superiority whose ideal form, the center by which displacement is measured, is 'God' (or 'Father'); this hydraulics guarantees
that whatever erection is currently being valorized will attain its
status by shifting the onus onto something metaphorized as
'female.' What is described here can, of course, be translated
without effort into explicitly Freudian terms; in fact, it suggests the
quintessence of the Oedipal dynamic as Freud lays it out, for a
man's allegiance *must* be shifted to the father, there *must* be infinite
deferment away from the mother. But, while the Oedipus Complex may institutionalize and thus extenuate misogyny, it cannot,
of course, be said to have initiated it within an historiographic
discourse whose allegorical consort is that ever-endangered virgin, Clio. The very system of sexual metaphors associated with
Our Lady of Historiography (and indeed with nicely draped
allegorical females in general) suggests that the approach-avoid-
ance waltz is nothing new. Freud's Oedipus Complex is one more
inevitable, if utterly influential, move within a language game
whose opportunistic misogyny had long since come to be felt as
supervalent.

And there is nothing essentialist at all about this deal (at least
not at the level of praxis) since the same metaphors do double
service, depending on to whom they are applied; anyone can be
tarred by this effeminate brush, and the historians with their eye
for detail, their love of material evidence, and their dependence
upon narrative (a form most congenial to the female's untutored
mind, a form embraced by armies of scribbling women) are in a
particularly high-risk category. The compromise formations
necessitated by historiography's putatively materialistic bias will
take their shapes opportunistically from whatever masculine/
feminine antithesis a given formulation generates, but, because
the historiographic process itself is grounded in assessment of
material detail, these readjustments are perpetual; a vertiginous

[18] David Musselwhite, *Partings Welded Together: Politics and Desire in the Nineteenth-
Century English Novel* (London: Methuen, 1987), 7.

dis-ease is built into the very system, which abnegates the glacial timeframe and the elevated perspective of philosophy even as it disdains the irresponsibilities of fictionalizing. In 'History and Psychoanalysis,' Dominick LaCapra speaks to historiography's double affiliation, 'Historians have traditionally accepted the Aristotelian stabilization of repetition / change by confiding in the binary opposition between the universal and the particular, between intemporal "synchrony" and changing "diachrony." In this decisive gesture, repetition is idealized and fixated on an ahistorical level while "history" is identified with change. This binary allows for a neat separation, if not isolation, of philosophy and history (with "poetry" as a rather unstable mediator or supplement between the two).'[19] Yet historiography's ambivalent relationship to philosophy *per se* is such that this negotiation becomes particularly energetic and complex, for the historian's commitment to materialities, to circumstantialities, to the diurnal and the mundane, his preoccupation with change and his recognition of himself and his text as inevitably and inextricably a part of what they do, all enforce a sense of an endless displacement from the ideal; in a lexicon whose inertia nudges words like 'materiality,' 'circumstantiality,' 'mundanity,' 'dailyness,' 'changeability,' and 'passivity' always away from the center of power and toward the chimera 'femaleness,' the historian has a ready-made job of compensation to perform. Consider, for example, what that man's man, Teddy Roosevelt, had to say about 'that preposterous little organization called I think the American Historical Association.' Roosevelt makes AHA historians, 'conscientious, industrious, painstaking little pedants,' seem less than men: 'Each of them was a good enough day laborer, trundling his barrowful of bricks and worthy of his hire; as long as they saw themselves as they were they were worth all respect; but when they imagined that by their activity they rendered the work of an architect unnecessary they became both absurd and mischievious.'[20]

Guild-work is built into the historian's conception of his role, but for a long while the only guilds remaining have been those, like altar-guilds, which prove the assimilation into 'femaleness' and domesticity of all the small works of days and hands, all the

[19] LaCapra, 'History and Psychoanalysis,' 12.
[20] Quoted in Howard K. Beale, 'The Professional Historian: His Theory and His Practice,' *Pacific Historical Review*, 22 (1953), 228.

work that is never, and can never be, done. The very archaism of this metaphor of the guild is telling, as if historians feel themselves at multiple and complex levels as things of the past, as members of a brotherhood many of whose members are dispersed into the larger workplace; it seems to imply that only some small few are left in the family business where work is still in some sense wholistic because it is downsized. And history is, of course, a perpetually unfinished business, a family business which must raise its men to the trade by making certain that all apron-strings are loosed; paradoxically, too, its very diurnal substantiality becomes the source of ambivalence within an oedipalized system that must distance itself from affiliations with womanliness. The historical brotherhood is forced to accommodate the paradox of its own self-claimed job description; engaged in a task that it consistently defines as unpretentious yeoman's labor in the muddy fields of material detail using the plainest language as its tool – if it were woman's work, it would be woman's work – it cultivates a self-deprecating pride and a certain filial diffidence relative to more grandiose systems. These responses concurrently produce the equal and opposite reaction by which such work is felt to be more honest, more commendable than the work of its high-flown brothers, the philosophers and the poets. And in this system Clio is a virgin, but women tend to get the rug pulled out from under them, time after time.

Within the historiographic system 'Woman' becomes for every historian the thing one must resist becoming; 'female,' what C. S. Lewis says all men are in the presence of God the Father, is the metamorphic spectre against which manhood holds its ground ('Divorce me,' says Donne to God, 'untie or break that knot again; / Take me to you, imprison me, for I, / Except you enthrall me, never shall be free, / Nor ever chaste, except you ravish me'); 'woman' is the desired and feared laxity – of language, of methodology, of truth-telling – against which the erection stands both as refutation and as impediment, with castration as much a fantasy as a phobia, like all anxiety compounded alchemically of desire and revulsion. Schreber is my medium within this fraught landscape, a name which has come to represent the quintessence of Oedipal tragedy through the drama of father and son, and a figure who articulates himself from *within* the explicit terms of this perpetual metamorphosis toward femaleness. 'Schreber,' the man-text of the *Memoirs* and a favorite subject of psychoanalytic and psychobiographical literature, resonates at every level of this discussion. He is the slight shudder at the heart of language and of sanity and of gender, a hermeneutic accident within which all other categories are destabilized.

Schreberian metaphysics

'This is the purpose of this manuscript; in it I shall try to give an at least partly comprehensible exposition of supernatural matters . . . I cannot of course count upon being *fully* understood because things are dealt with which cannot be expressed in human language; they exceed human understanding. Nor can I maintain that *everything* is irrefutably certain, even for me: much remains only presumption and probability.'[21] Schreber speaks for many of us who write, and certainly he speaks here for me; literary critics and historians and philosophers and theologians echo him as they begin the oxymoronic task of making the crooked straight without in the process losing the crooked complexities they have come to expose. Because he functions within an unequivocal metaphysics, he confesses from the beginning that his production of language is always a displacement from the dream of Truth: 'To make myself at least somewhat comprehensible,' he says, 'I shall have to speak much in images and similes, which may at times perhaps be only *approximately* correct; for the only way a human being can make supernatural matters, which in their essence must always remain incomprehensible, understandable to a certain degree is by comparing them with known facts of human experience. Where intellectual understanding ends, the domain of belief begins; man must reconcile himself to the fact that things exist which are true although he cannot understand them'(41). In this claim for truth, Schreber is only more candid in his fantasy than most, and in his claim for the necessity of a language that is tropic rather than straight he is merely less ingenuous than those who proselytize for a clean, transparent, metaphor-free narrative.

Institutionalized, suffering, Schreber writes under more than ordinary duress, but, still, his dilemma is the hyperbole by which

---

[21] Daniel Paul Schreber, *Memoirs of My Nervous Illness*, trans. ed., Ida Macalpin and Richard Hunter (London: Dawson and Sons, 1955), 41. All further references to this text will be cited parenthetically.

we may measure our own relationship to language as we work to make it speak for some truth. His is the limit-condition case by which the slippage between language and its association to 'meaning,' 'truth,' 'reality,' and all those other lost centers may be measured, for he *lives* in that barrierless and vertiginous place between fiction and fact, hallucination and material reality. His candor and his madness reveal, in hyperbolic measure, the dis-ease that comes with attempting to articulate the real and the true: his is the textbook case by which more ordinary pathologies may be measured, and this in other than Freudian terms. He feels his lexicon as bivalent, produced from within and from without, both a matter of choice and of inspiration; the 'so-called "basic language"' that fills his *Memoirs* provides him with a set of terms from 'the language spoken by God himself,' and yet he uses these words with authority, weaving them into his text so that they become his own (49-50). Conscious of his treacherous placement physically and mentally, he is forced to judgments relative to the 'real' that language, so graciously ambiguous and so richly tropological, more easily displaces or defers among the non-institutionalized and the poets. Recognizing that his semantic field is a matter of negotiation, he modifies his terms with 'so-called,' thus bringing to the fore just how tenuous are our definitions, and how arbitrary. Forced to confront his equivocal location, he must struggle to separate the 'real visions . . . that is the dream-images produced by rays' from 'mere hallucinations' (89-90). 'In my opinion,' he says speaking for poets, theologians, and philosophers as well as for madmen, 'science would go very wrong to designate as "hallucinations" *all* such phenomena that lack objective reality, and to throw them into the lumber room of things that do not exist'(90). Schreber struggles with phantasms, and in some measure so do we all.

Schreber tells a story that taps in its hearers a great reservoir of existential anxiety; his madness is too close for comfort to the visionary, too close to the threat or promise of an apocalyptic barrierlessness where all conventional distinctions between man and woman and people and things erode and the body itself comes to be felt as prosthetic. Freud premised that schizophrenia is marked by a slippage of conventional relationships between words and things; and when the Freudian equation, itself complex and provocative, enters the vortex of the linguistic turn where conventional relationships between words and things are de-stabilized, one may more clearly see in schizophrenic speech the limit conditions of our own troubled romance with realism. Freud observes in schizophrenia 'a predominance of what has to do with words over what has to do with things,' so that resemblances are seen, not among things, but among the words that describe them (squeezing blackheads and ejaculation, 'spurting'); the schizophrenic mode of thought, then, is to treat 'concrete things as though they were abstract.'[22] Or to say it another way, to treat abstract things – words – as if they were concrete, to proceed as if words were themselves things, weighty and material. Figurative paradise or nightmare, this condition accords language full performative status: word-things whose naming is as definitive and arbitrary as a bottle of champagne exploding against a ship's prow. And yet, even as it blurs the demarcations between words and things, this Schreberian condition enforces by virtue of its own evident suffering their inexorable differences.

Schreber must try to find and to articulate what will pass as objectively real, and in his sensitized condition he discovers at a most visceral level what poets learn early on: that language always reciprocates materiality's insistence upon itself with a metonymous force of its own. If we are to some extent formed by our surroundings and begin to see and to articulate ourselves as contiguous extensions of our obligations, our workplace, our tools, and our texts, we also project internalities onto the material landscape, making the world conform to inner topographies. As they are spoken, things lose parts of themselves, are aggrandized or diminished synechdocally, and are assimilated into surrounding contiguities and made more, or less, than themselves. Barthes calls this the *'the spitefulness of language'*: 'in order to *utter* itself,' he says, 'the total body must revert to the dust of words, to the listing of details, to a monotonous inventory of parts, to crumbling: language undoes the body, returns it to the fetish.'[23] One need not, of course, see this anatomizing as insufficiency; the fetish is, after all, a powerful stimulant, and the enumeration of parts may provoke a less than desiccated response, as Petrarch and Sade both

[22] Sigmund Freud, 'The Unconscious,' in *The Standard Edition of the Complete Psychological Works*, ed. James Strachey (London: Hogarth Press, 1964), 200.

[23] Roland Barthes, *S/Z: An Essay*, trans. Richard Miller (New York: Farrar, Straus and Giroux, 1974), 113.

knew. But because things *must* be spoken, for the most part, one can only distinguish Schreber's metamorphic intuitions and his metonymic sensibilities by their intensity and not their kind.

For Schreber, metonymies actualize themselves in a constant reciprocity among material states; his language exposes the seams between what is 'real' – that is, what is sanctioned – and what is hallucinatory. He speaks and sees within the surreal venue of the madhouse, where the monstrous is not only to be found within the catachreses of asylum-talk, but is also disposed within the bodies of tormented patients – his own, with its inexplicable contortions and refusals, and others' – and lies as well within the instruments of restraint, the salts and bromides and tinctures, within the very walls and bars. As with everyday language, one is often hard-pressed in reading the *Memoirs* to distinguish between accurate reporting, figurative speech, and madness; added to these ambiguities must be the demonstrable connection between Schreber's language and his father's dictums, between Schreber's apprehension of a world of bodies prosthetically constructed and his father's imposition on him of straps, halters, rods, and cuffs. There are times, as Niederland and Schatzman point out, that he is merely being literal. If, then, Schreber speaks the schizophrenic's body language, what Freud calls 'organ-speech,' he also clarifies metonymy's reductionisms, its palpable instinct for contiguities. 'In schizophrenia,' says Freud, '*words* are subjected to the same process as that which makes the dream images out of latent dream thoughts . . . They undergo condensation, and by means of displacement transfer their cathexes to one another in their entirety. The process may go so far that a single word, if it is specially suitable on account of its numerous connections, takes over the representation of a whole train of thought.'[24] This is, of course, the way figurative language works as well, and the distinction between whether such linguistic processes are deemed symptomatic of madness or of artistry lies in the specific ways in which the real is adjudicated within text and context.

Schreber works to articulate a bridge between what he senses to be the radical incommensurability between God's basic language – that which is revealed to him alone – and an entire series of common discourses with which he is familiar and which he knows

[24] Freud, 'The Unconscious,' 199.

to be acceptably sane: medical, juridical, poetic, domestic, political, etc. Messianic, he opens himself fully to metonymy's imperialistic claiming of space. He apprehends himself as neither here nor there: neither autonomous nor automaton, neither man nor woman, neither dead nor alive, but always in dangerous or pleasurable flux between extremes, with organs disappearing, poisons ebbing and flowing, rays attacking and receding. Bodies elide into things and into other bodies – more than once he sees his roommate 'becoming one with his bed,' and he repeatedly witnesses people changing heads with each other in the common room (104-05). His own body suffers and enjoys a perpetual, asymptotic progress toward becoming female. Even 'lifeless objects' miracle themselves into new things: 'However skeptical I try to be now in scrutinizing my recollections,' he says, 'I cannot erase certain impressions from my memory, in which I saw even articles of clothing on the bodies of human beings being transformed, as well as food on my plate during meals (for instance, pork into veal or vice versa)' (107). Equally transubstantiative, his body suffers an inexplicable physiology of decay and regeneration; a Beckett character, he feels as if pieces of himself are likely to drop off or disappear or go dead. Schreber, divested of the easy complacencies of normalcy, reticulates the poetic and the actual, the phantasmatic and the historical, the hyperbolic and the truthful in ways that at once expose the joints between them (because he is mad) and prove them less oppositional than akin.

On the other hand, Schreber knows the feel of the straitjacket, can taste the sting of potassium bromide on his tongue: materiality often bites back and does not listen to explanations or take into account extenuating circumstance. There is mute reality – the space in which one lives and breathes and moves – that is and does at the same moment, with the instant of recognition, if an instant is afforded at all, only the space of the guillotine's fall. As Clement Rosset says, 'Reality situates its sentence at the very level of execution from the start.'[25] This laconic real refutes language even as it provokes one to attempt its taxonomy. Flannery O'Connor, for example, makes this infinitesimal moment of unspeakable recognition – perhaps it is grace, but it is at least sudden and ephemeral meaning – more than ordinarily clear. One thinks, for

[25] Clement Rosset, *Joyful Cruelty: Toward a Philosophy of the Real*, trans. David F. Bell (New York: Oxford University Press, 1993), 77.

example, of the grandmother and the Misfit in 'A Good Man is Hard to Find,' of how she speaks, and like any of us can *only* speak, a language of banality and cliché right up to the point where grace and a bullet to the chest arrive in a single epiphany. If Schreber is in the thrall of a capricious, unseen holiness, he also lives within the walls of an asylum whose barriers do not give way before his thoughts; confined in a darkened cell, he learns the lessons of impenetrability – 'As long as the shutters were closed I often thundered against them with my fists until my hands were raw; once I succeeded in knocking a shutter down by force which had already been loosened by miracle, with the result that the cross-bar was by miracle made to descend on my head with such force that my head and my chest were covered with blood'(163). Guillotine or window-sash, one still runs the Shandian risk of being lopped off before one can utter a word.

But, short of such catastrophes of grace, one is most usually left to babble a world into place and to keep it there through various versions of fast-talk; in fact, as O'Connor's habit of the teleological *coup de grâce* makes clear, if one survives to speak again he will inevitably return to talking trash. Schreber communicates the sense that as long as one may speak, words and things will remain reciprocal, their relationship restless (this equation of course excludes the extremes at both ends, the language of authoritarianism or totalitarianism and certain violent or pernicious materialities); he proves that this reciprocity is not negligible, not merely the fancy talk of literary critics and theoreticians, as he writes and argues his way over the threshold from catatonia to full suffrage. He proves, both legally and poetically, that, although things may have an irrefutable material presence, words, with their constative, rhetorical, and performative force, may alter as well as be influenced by materialities.

Schreber's language takes place on this fault line, this misfit between material and linguistic energies. From a meta-textual perspective the *Memoirs* is sylleptically constructed of two simultaneous meanings. One great pun on the double meaning of 'Truth' straddles the text: Schreber tells the truth, and it is not the truth; Schreber is utterly believable, and he is completely unreliable. One must have quick feet to dodge the cracks in the floor as they open up. Language is, says, Heidegger, the house of Being, but Schreber proves that one may articulate himself an asylum – a safehouse and a madhouse at the same time; language, in Schreber's case, creates a self for which Being is for once quite clearly constituted by its very disintegrative status and shown to be as tenuous a prospect as Heidegger would have had it. He must speak and be heard in order to Be, and in speaking he undoes himself as all but a madman, divesting himself of all the conventional and prefabricated edifices – juridical, sexual, political, and otherwise – in which personhood may more comfortably house itself. In these houses, where discourses are in place and there are always surrogates to speak, one may be silent, but Schreber knows that as he is unique he is also perpetually endangered. He makes this intuition quite explicit, for his terror of 'thinking nothing' – of letting his mind go empty of sound and thought – lies in his conviction that wordlessness is the surest and fastest way for the soul murderers to take him over once and for all. So he bellows and sings and bangs interminably on the piano, using sound to keep the soul murderers out of the house. Scheherezadic, he senses that language is all that keeps him in the world, all that keeps the assassins preoccupied enough to let him live one more hour, one more day. His exigency regarding the disjunctive work of speaking the truth is extreme; but it may nonetheless be said to reveal a problem also shared by the putatively sane.

Schreber may be mad, but he is not an amnesiac, and he remembers and remains informed by his performance of the tasks relative to language that pushed him over the edge into sleeplessness and acute suffering; the crucial fact that he argued himself out of the asylum adds yet another layer, for it is an historical detail that works retroactively to shift his *Memoirs* into an even more complex register. He was a judge, a politician, a Senatspräsident presiding over other judges, a man in and of the world performing the multiple obligations of a full and manly citizenry. From the beginning of his appointment he felt his complex negotiations between action and justification as crucial: 'On the 1st of October 1893 I took up office as *Senatspräsident* to the Superior Court in Dresden. I have already mentioned the heavy burden of work I found there. I was driven, maybe by personal ambition, but certainly also in the interests of the office, to achieve first of all the necessary respect among my colleagues and others concerned with the Court (barristers, etc.) by unquestionable efficiency'(63). He was both powerful, as presiding judge, and vulnerable: 'The task was all the heavier and demanded all the more tact in my personal dealings with the members of the panel of five Judges over which I had to preside, as almost all of them were much senior (up to twenty years), and anyway they were much more intimately acquainted with the procedure of the Court, to which I was a newcomer'(63–64). Schreber, in fact, is not just any old madman, but one uniquely qualified to testify to the complexities of a language used to discover 'truth,' pronounce judgment, persuade, and mobilize. Judge Schreber (retired), who knows first-hand that judgments must be pronounced regardless of ambiguities, inmate Schreber, who knows first-hand that judgments *are* pronounced regardless of ambiguities, becomes prophet Schreber because he has fallen into that interstitial space where the two modes join themselves. But ordinary language, and those of us who speak it, stand just on either side of this space.

So, although his is a most complex language game in which the stakes are very, very high, it is also utterly commensurable with a kind of game more generally played (alternatively, in some ways not to be considered here, it may not exist at all except in very loose translations which, because of Schreber's (non)status as a madman, need not fear accountability; as Wittgenstein says, 'If a lion could talk, we would not understand him'). Moreover, we have every reason to feel that Schreber is working to speak truth; within an impeccable system, logically inclined, using terms that are clearly defined and consistently deployed, Schreber makes his case. And thus, in this intensification of the necessity to make words testify, Schreber's *Memoirs* may speak about language in ways that it might not be licensed from the outside to speak about a 'sane' external reality. And it speaks about *our* language outside the asylum walls, because it reveals the hallucinogenesis of language. Tropologically inclined toward metaphor and simile, not to mention metonymy, syllepsis, oxymoron and multiple other twists, language has an inertial force that Schreber's text only more palpably recognizes.

His language is a fully enriched product: it is performative in the sense that it enacts part of his own curative program and in that it also moves the courts toward rescission of his tutelage; it is poetic and theological in that it seeks to reveal God and truth; it is pedagogical in that it would teach others what Schreber has learned through hard experience; it is rhetorically sophisticated in that Schreber knows full well that his diagnosis – 'madman,' for short – necessitates the most careful and persuasive of logic, the clearest of expositions, the most compelling use of detail and evidence; and it is compulsively truthful – the partial undoing of all of the above – for Schreber's mania diverts him from the euphemistic, paraphrastic, and circumlocutionary means by which he might cover what he knows will be seen as his excessive convictions (had he been able to do this, he would have been a novelist or a poet). So it is Schreber who bellows in the background of this book. A figure who falls into language from various states of grace and damnation, a figure who sometimes explodes under the peremptory urgings of the bellowing miracle into sheer, inchoate sound, a figure who is, in my eyes, as heroic in the face of an assaultive madness as there ever could be. Crazy Schreber makes a good patron saint for a literary critic, because if he feels the tragic insufficiency of his writing in the face of a painfully real existence, he is also comic and knows himself to be – he often sees the macabre humor in his situation and feels the whimsy of his basic language. He is a nice reminder of one's own thoroughly compromised position relative to any given process of evaluation, and he is a particularly salutary figure to keep in mind when the father, as he inevitably does, rears his head.

2

❖❖❖

Strange angels: negation and performativity

❖❖❖

This is how one pictures the angel of history. His face is turned toward the past. Where we perceive a chain of events, he sees one single catastrophe which keeps piling wreckage upon wreckage and hurls it in front of his feet. The angel would like to stay, awaken the dead, and make whole what has been smashed. But a storm is blowing in from Paradise; it has got caught in his wings with such violence that the angel can no longer close them. The storm irresistibly propels him into the future to which his back is turned, while the pile of debris before him grows skyward.

Walter Benjamin, 'Theses on the Philosophy of History,' IX[1]

Negation

To state the case again briefly: the psychohistorians re-enact the Oedipal dramas by which they shape their narratives; they reify within their texts the amnesiac necessities of the successfully Oedipalized by working within the terms of an external authority ('psychoanalysis') whose dicta they follow even as they resist – through the normalizing of language, the resistance to 'jargon,' etc. – full assimilation to its point of view. Yet, ironically, the historians who speak of themselves as unregenerate or unapologetic traditionalists and who either disdainfully ignore or who repudiate psychohistory in order to guard the simple purities of historical discourse, are the more successfully socialized (the very fact that psychohistory is a marginal discipline speaks worlds about both sides); their conflictual relationship to the terms of their craft disperses its energies within the allowable boundaries of the

---

[1] Walter Benjamin, *Illuminations: Essays and Reflections*, ed. Hannah Arendt (New York: Schocken Books, 1968), 257. For the lyrical contexts in which this may be read, see Carolyn Forche's use of this epigraph in her book of poetry, *The Angel of History* (New York: HarperCollins Publishers, 1994), and Laurie Anderson's use of the same image in 'Strange Angels.'

Oedipal dynamic, but because traditional historiography does not explicitly mobilize the Oedipus Complex as an explanatory model one may be left with the illusion that the anxieties of influence that affect crucial choices – evidential, discursive, analytic – are localized and containable. If the psychohistorians are, as their opponents suggest, in the thrall of a powerful outside influence called 'psychoanalysis,' the historian who upholds the historiographic tradition of clear, unmetaphorized narrative produced through objective assessments of evidence and in the service of truth is similarly bound to a kind of forgetfulness. Memory becomes a virtually talismanic concept in historical discourse, perhaps because that discourse is haunted by a memory of the alternative truths one must necessarily exclude to produce 'truth.'

Oedipalized responsiveness allows for a merciful respite from the competing imperatives within traditional historiography: imperatives to be true, but without speaking metaphysically, to be within time and above it, to be materially and evidentially bound without succumbing to positivism, to be perceptually sophisticated about materialities without yielding to idealist paranoias. For it licenses, indeed it demands, forgetting. Central to Freud's formulation of Oedipal anxiety is the phantasmatic knife, and not as in poetry to produce the fruitful obstetrics of caesura, not to cut so as to release the analogic, figurative, or rhythmic potentials of the poetic line. This knife is for castration: it is as if Freud in a single nightmare vision sums up an entire western discourse for which the antithesis to moderate virility is emasculation, as if it is an anxiety dream one might have the night before a book report on Aristotle's *Nicomachean Ethics*. If there was ever a threat to authorize one's giving in to rules of law, this is it, this knife poised above soft flesh; an image conceived to bind wish fulfillment and the punishment for that wish in a single tight knot, the castration fantasy – that which might make one a woman, the good and the bad news – is redolent with inherited possibility. (Such a shared hallucination might make an Oedipal believer out of me, for instance, if I only had a penis to worry about, and there, as they say, is the rub.) It is not inconsequential that traditional historians are so often dressed down by theorists and philosophers; these historians make ordinarily circumspect people irascible because they communicate a disjunctiveness between expectation and procedure which the rest of us share but seem to feel far more miserable about. There is in conventional historiography, one feels, a set of recognitions oriented toward the act of uttering (one's own and others') and a set of recognitions oriented toward the utterance itself, and between the two lies Aporia, like some bemused goddess of forgetfulness.

Barthes' 'The Discourse of History' puts this in extremist terms:

> The historical fact is linguistically associated with a privileged ontological status: we recount what has been, not what has not been, or what has been uncertain. To sum up, historical discourse is not acquainted with negation (or only very rarely, in exceptional cases). Strangely enough, but significantly, this fact can be compared with the tendency which we find in a type of utterer who is very different from the historian: that is, the psychotic, who is incapable of submitting an utterance to a negative transformation. We can conclude that, in a certain sense, 'objective' discourse (as in the case of positivist history) shares the situation of schizophrenic discourse. In both cases there is a radical censorship of the act of uttering (which has to be experienced for a negative transformation to take place), a massive flowing back of discourse in the direction of the utterance and even (in the historian's case) in the direction of the referent: no one is there to take responsibility for the utterance.[2]

This is, of course, a rather hyperbolic analogy which may be more provocative than accurate in its assertion of the affiliation between 'objective' history-writing and psychosis (Joan Scott's more temperate assertion in *Gender and the Politics of History* regarding negation tames the implications of this observation[3]). But in its outrageous linking of historians and schizophrenics, Barthes' assessment provokes the more interesting possibility that any avowedly non-fictional, non-lyrical discourse must proceed by a series of what amount to psychotic breaks, the systemic tolerance of ambiguity, contradiction, and uncertainty in constant tension with moments of willful redirection back toward the utterance and the referent: if there is an element of the pot calling the kettle black in psychohistoriographic work on Schreber, and if 'objective' history shares the schizophrenic's forgetfulness of competing possibilities for truth, this objectivity psychosis is also a more generalizable delusion, one in which the only remedy, always partial, is acknowledgment.

[2] Roland Barthes. 'The Discourse of History,' trans. Stephen Bann, in *Comparative Criticism: A Yearbook*, ed. E. S. Shaffer (Cambridge University Press, 1981), 14.

[3] Joan W. Scott, *Gender and the Politics of History* (New York: Columbia University Press, 1988), 6.

In thinking about this matter of conventional historiography, then, the division is not to be made between the enlightened (those invariably sensitive to the interdependencies of the utterance and the act of uttering) and the self-deluded (in Barthes' formulation the psychotic and the positivist historian); the distinction is not gross but subtle, having to do with the limiting conditions for negotiations between concepts of objectivity and subjectivity within a given discourse. Neither is the distinction between a discourse whose internal logic is impeccable and one fraught with illogic and contradiction, for any system worth speaking of will be so multivalent as to destabilize a purely logical structure: the meta-text will never cover all of the exigencies of the specific texts from which it has been derived. When these stark oppositions are left aside, the demarcations of differences are at once more subtle and less satisfyingly definitive. But, in fact, the question, which assumes the risk of its own fineshadedness within overarching deconstructionist truisms even as it claims a certain pragmatic advantage, should be this: given the stated logical and method-ological predispositions of a discourse, where are the points of internal contradiction and how much anxiety does this produce *within the discourse itself*? How close is the knife felt to be? (Or another way of putting this: how necessary is the fantasy of the knife?) Do the expectations of a broadly defined conventional historiography, predicated on the Rankean dictum to tell what actually happened, exist from the beginning within a larger discursive field whose challenge is in some way overweening (does, in fact, the Rankean dictum come about *because* of this challenge, a simultaneous adjustment and resistance to an atmos-phere that also produces a Hegelian philosophy of history)? And is the historiographic undertaking therefore more than ordinarily susceptible to this 'psychosis' by which objectivity is claimed through the repudiation of other levels of knowledge; is it, in other words, Oedipally overdetermined?

'History' is already a destabilized term which, purporting to cover both the thing itself – the material manifestations of events in time – and the texts that discover it, in fact occupies the unclaimed ground in between; it becomes, as do so many other words ('aesthetic,' for example, or 'sublimity,' or 'human nature') a metonymy for an entire network of contiguous events and rela-tionships without which it could not come into existence, while also, irresistibly, seeming to concretize two specific things, 'history' – what happened out there, and 'history' – the story of those events. But, while a word like 'aesthetic' authorizes its liminal placement by virtue of what it claims to be – i.e. beauty, and not goodness or truth, and in Kantean terms a subjective rather than an objective universality and non-existent except as it is perceived – 'history' does the opposite. It names two systems, and historians' qualifications and modesties notwithstanding, it suggests that the one history, the discourse, will be the Cinderella slipper for the other history, out there waiting to be claimed. Clio walks only by virtue of these magic shoes; 'realness,' what actually happened, can and must be tracked down, shod, and given a name.

An obligation to the real is a heavy burden even when one sustains the illusion of standing apart from it as an observer, but the non-positivist, putatively non-metaphysical historian knows himself to be *inside* the terms of what he does; that narrative is promoted as the necessary medium through which history is revealed suggests the historian's sense of placement, intuitive or claimed, within a dense, infinitely extended field of reference, just as it further suggests his sense, intuitive or claimed, that the *telos* must be manufactured, that a point must be chosen as in some crucial way initiatory. Articulating this paradox of infinite extension and arbitrary closure, the poet James Merrill says of prose, 'I persist in seeing it as a mildly nightmarish medium, to which *there is no end*: conterminous with one's very life . . . With prose, as I saw it, the aria never came. All was recitative which, however threatened by resolution, continued self-importantly to advance the plot, explaining, describing, discriminating.'[4] The historian, by virtue of his avowed responsibilities to a causally complex field of evidence, cannot claim to have begun his discourse by yielding to absolute necessity (thus, as Barthes says, the difficulty in historical texts of the exordium) but must instead proceed reflexively, so that the license for beginning is a question already located within a rich texture of time and space – 'Why now?'[5] One's response to the aesthetic or the sublime does not suffer this element of arbitrary choice, for, while one may be more or less susceptible to aesthetic conditions or to sublimity, it is the *fact* of a response felt as inevitable and externally motivated that defines the terms. Indeed,

---

[4] James Merrill, *Recitative* (San Francisco: North Point Press, 1986), Foreword.
[5] Roland Barthes, 'The Discourse of History,' 9.

to avoid the implication of outside influences, the historian explicitly repudiates 'poetry' in his own language, which must abnegate its preoccupation with itself in favor of its obligation to translate realness as faithfully and with as much clarity as possible. The Muses of Poetry, for example, are bad influences on men who would remain rational and committed to truth. 'Who . . . has allowed these hysterical sluts to approach this sick man's bedside?' storms the Muse of Philosophy as she stands by Boethius' side, 'They have no medicine to ease his pains, only sweetened poison to make them worse. These are the very women who kill the rich and fruitful harvest of Reason with the barren thorns of Passion. They habituate men to their sickness of mind instead of curing them.'[6] Clio, says Barzun, must be protected from the quacks and isolated from the more promiscuous Muses, even as she must be constantly examined by the good doctors of history to see that she remains *virga intacta.*[7]

The historian embraces unadorned narrative prose as the necessary antithesis to poetic license and licentiousness, for to be prosaic by virtue of being concerned with the prosaic – the daily, the particular, the real – is to recognize history rather than self. 'As it reaches down into the foundations of language as "taking place," prose can make allowance for the speech within it,' write Kittay and Godzich in *The Emergence of Prose*:

Put differently: once having worked out the basic problem and mechanisms of deixis (how language connects itself with what is under it), prose can pretend to be both language and what is under it. This is what a body cannot do: a body relies upon deixis, uses it, but does not constitute it. Prose can *hold* speech. Speech cannot hold prose.

Or put another way, prose can embody history's particulars, encompass all of the individual, idiosyncratic, speaking bodies that die off and reproduce; just as it *has* a history, prose is best equipped to perform the multiple infoldings that constitute (that) history. 'Prose can situate itself in a foundational position with respect to all language. It will under-stand and under-write speech and verse. But it will not display such understanding,

---

[6] Boethius, *The Consolation of Philosophy*, trans. V. E. Watts (New York: Penguin, 1969), 36.

[7] Jacques Barzun, *Clio and the Doctors: Quanto-History, Psycho-History, and History* (University of Chicago Press, 1974), 158.

which would only bring it out of the background that is its ground.'[8]

Yet prose deployed within the exigencies of narrative slips from its meta-textual status toward the poetry and speech it contains. Even fictional realism, which cushions realness within the softer boundaries of make-believe, has to work hard to make the true facts stick so that they also hold their meanings as real elements of historical time and place. Even fictional realism struggles with the paradox of ordering and closure, whereby teleological necessities both external and internal are felt as in conflict with the alternative 'realness' of disorder and extensiveness. This dilemma is over-determined within historical narrative, where the ratio is reversed, and factual, evidentially verifiable material is meant so thoroughly to infiltrate the narrative matrix as to wrest it away from its propensities toward story-telling and back toward 'objectively' verifiable truth. The concept of objectivity, when divested of its metaphysical underpinnings, may be pragmatically useful within a discourse that has need of it as a way of orienting language use, of determining appropriate affect for a given situation, and of setting parameters, but it is pure trouble in a system whose double allegiances are to extreme temporal, chronological, and material specificity, on the one hand, and to textual negotiations which shape these specificities into language that works to meet unde-fined but implicit criteria for truth statements, on the other.

The historian, by definition of his disciplinary and epis-temological affiliations, is thus more than ordinarily enmeshed within his own initializing narrative, with neither the comforts of claimed fictionality nor the systematic isolationism available to philosophical discourse. The critic of a realist novel may say of the author that she writes fiction but communicates as well 'history'; Stephen Gill says, for example, of Eliot's fiction, 'Reading the novel is a process of learning simultaneously about the world of Adam Bede and the world of *Adam Bede.*'[9] This formulation allows for an historical communication that is, because secondary and oblique to the realist fiction from which it exudes itself, more atmospheric than actualized: history and biography as osmosis, that teeming present which the author has assimilated infusing itself into our present through an absorbative process. The philos-

[8] Jeffrey Kittay and Wlad Godzich, *The Emergence of Prose: An Essay in Prosaics* (Minneapolis: University of Minnesota Press, 1987), 198.

[9] George Eliot, *Adam Bede*, intro. Stephen Gill (New York: Penguin, 1985), 22.

opher, on the other hand, may distinguish between the kind of metalanguages he chooses to employ; a metalanguage in the linguist's sense will mean that he will make the phrases of the texts themselves the object of his inquiry; a metalanguage in the logician's sense means that he will attempt to constitute the grammar of an object-language.[10] In the case of the former, the philosopher can imagine himself as discoursing at a purely reflective, 'philosophical' level which does not proceed by a set of presupposed rules (whether he can actually do this is not the question but the fact that his discipline licenses him to employ this strategy). In any case, philosophical discourse *by virtue of what it is* will always be licensed, indeed required, to promote a conceptual scheme even if, as with Donald Davidson, this constitutes itself as exploding the very idea of a conceptual scheme; if it is experientially derived it will be nonetheless self-enclosed. The brain is its metonymy. Philosophy says, with Emily Dickinson, 'The brain – is wider than the Sky / For – put them side by side – / The one the other will contain / With ease – and You – beside – .' For philosophy, 'The Brain is just the weight of God,' but history's commitment is outward, into the world of time and place. It is as if 'history' sublates itself from the two poles of fiction and philosophy, rising out of the oxymorons of fictional truth (the realistic novel) and true lies (philosophy).

The historian's obligations are to avoid the fictional and to bracket or repudiate the metaphysical: to get down in the muck of dailiness and detail without succumbing to chaos or violating the truth of this multiplicity through excessive systematization or exclusion. Collingwood's claim is thus neither unique nor archaic: the idea which governs the historian's work 'is clear, rational, and universal. It is the idea of the historical imagination as a self-dependent, self-determining, and self-justifying form of thought.'[11] In Lyotard's formulation, the historian is bound sequentially in such a way as to make a metadiscourse impossible:

Phrases form a physical universe if they are grasped as moving objects which form a finite series. The phrase referring to this universe is therefore by hypothesis part of that universe: it will become part of it in the following instant. If we call history the series of phrases considered in

---

[10] See Jean-François Lyotard, *The Differend: Phrases in Dispute*, trans. Georges Van Den Abbeele (Minneapolis: University of Minnesota Press, 1988), xiv.

[11] R. G. Collingwood, *The Idea of History*, ed. Jan Van Der Dussen (Oxford: Clarendon Press, 1993), 249.

this way (physically), then the historian's phrase 'will become part' of the universe to which it refers. The difficulties raised by historicism and dogmatism stem from this situation. The former declares that his phrase is part of its referent, history; the latter that his phrase is not part of it.[12]

In the historicist formulation as it is represented here, the historian, who sees his language as vital, productive, material in weight and effect, must feel its coming forth as history and must recognize that his phrasal system not only pours forth to join its referent, history, but is also actually pulled forth by the inertial energy of that referent. This is the serpent's tail down its throat, History swallowing itself, and a problem only if one chokes on the anti-metaphysical implications of the snack. The dogmatist's alternative formulation – that his phrase does not become part of the referent, history – suggests that one makes, and means to make, another history, this one 'true,' or 'accurate' in a way that the non-dogmatic historicist must abjure. And this is only a problem if one maintains one of the basic premises of historiography: that there is a necessary and verifiable connection to be sustained between the physical universe about which the historian speaks and the words that bespeak that universe.

Lyotard's assertions may be felt, at least by historians, to be born of the philosopher's, the theoretician's, and the Frenchman's arrogance and his removal from and lack of experience with real, tangible events within time, but Collingwood speaks in a way that is consonant with Lyotard's less friendly resistance to the historian's claims. Collingwood's essay, 'Some Perplexities About Time: With an Attempted Solution,' brings some of these paradoxes within historiography powerfully to the fore. He works to wrestle misconceptions to the ground: 'My central difficulty is this: – *All statements ordinarily made about time seem to imply that time is something which we know it is not, and make assumptions about it which we know to be untrue.'*[13] The past and the future are not real, he says, for time can only be known as 'a perpetually changing present'; the past doesn't continue to exist, 'What does continue to exist is the contribution it has made to the present.'[14] There is in his apprehension of time a powerful sense of contiguity, whereby 'infinity' becomes 'only a metaphorical phrase to describe the

[12] Lyotard, *The Differend*, 7.
[13] R. G. Collingwood, 'Some Perplexities about Time,' *Proceedings of the Aristotelian Society*, vol. 26 (1925–26), 138.   [14] *Ibid.*, 144.

infinite complexity of that one event which is the history of the world.'[15] He goes on: 'I shall therefore assume that an event takes time and is always (i) part of an event which takes more time, (ii) divisible into elements that take less; and that events are in no sense composed of instant or point-instants but always of events. Time is therefore . . . to be sought *within* events, not in the relations *between* events, except so far as these relations fall within larger events.'[16] Collingwood refers in this essay to his own experience as an historian, and makes it clear that, while his discourse for the *Proceedings of the Aristotelian Society* may be philosophical in orientation, his understanding of time is derived from his sense of how history works. More inclined to paradox than many historians, Collingwood is nonetheless a fairly representative spokesman of a certain version of historiographic time. And feeling themselves embedded and entangled within the syntagma of a past extending unbroken into the present, historians will also be driven back to a legitimizing fiction whose source is theological, however disguised or distant that version of Presence might be. 'History,' the name for that thing between language and materiality, projects itself in the oxymoronic terms of the absent or past present it brings forth; neither here nor there, it awakens a curious suspicion of absence.

Barthes' assertion that historical discourse is 'not acquainted with negation' becomes in this context a provocative way of speaking of this gap: 'negation,' another exceedingly enriched concept which infiltrates and underpins philosophical, literary, and psychoanalytic discourse, is one way of getting at the questions of judgment raised by a consideration of Oedipal imperatives. 'Negation' is, in Freud's use of the term, fraught with complexity, as it affords a means of bringing into language but not into full recognition a truth that is repressed, and of bringing into consciousness some sense that assertions felt as truth may be challenged legitimately from without; it is, says Freud, the very basis of our capacity to form judgments, as it proves that one may evaluate the justice of an assertion at some level other than that of pure affect. (Negation: 'Procedure whereby the subject, while formulating one of his wishes, thoughts or feelings which has been repressed hitherto, contrives, by disowning it, to continue to

---

[15] *Ibid.*, 143.   [16] Collingwood, 'Some Perplexities,' 137.

defend himself against it.'[17]) Negation is not so simple a phenomenon as the caricatured formulations would suggest, for, while it is true that an analysand's volunteering the statement, 'I don't hate my mother,' will be heard by the therapist as *also* expressing the unutterable opposite, it is also true that the analysand (or indeed anyone sensitive to language and truth claims) may be brought through reflection on this process to an intellectual awareness of, even a belief in, its alternative and denied content, a belief which never, however, completely mitigates the repression itself by being *felt* as equally true: 'Negation is a way of taking cognizance of what is repressed; indeed, it is already a lifting of the repression, though not, of course, an acceptance of what is repressed. We can see how in this the intellectual function is separated from the affective process,' says Freud.[18]

In other words, to be 'acquainted with negation,' as Barthes puts it, is to come to recognize through discourse itself that the act of uttering distorts the utterance, that there is an inevitable anamorphosis even in the most 'truthful' of statements, because truth always carries within it, also as truth, the potential or actuality of its own negation. This is what allows for reality testing and for a demarcation between internal and external truths by assessing where they match up and where they diverge.[19] The choice, one begins to see, is not between true and false – for 'I don't hate my mother' is in crucial ways very true – but between externally verifiable, accepted, workable, semantically efficient truthfulness and its more inchoate counterpart; negation reveals the necessarily arbitrary nature of language. 'The performance of the function of judgment is not made possible,' says Freud, 'until the creation of the symbol of negation has endowed thinking with a first measure of freedom from the consequences of repression and, with it, from the compulsion of the pleasure principle'; 'since to affirm or negate the content of thoughts is the task of the function of intellectual judgement' this leads to 'the psychological origin of that function.'[20] One who is 'acquainted with negation' would recognize the full implications of a capacity – indeed, a virtual mechanism – by which one may *know* unknowability; 'acquainted' here would

[17] J. Laplanche and J.-B. Pontalis, *The Language of Psychoanalysis*, trans. Donald Nicholson Smith (New York: W. W. Norton & Co., 1973), 261–63.
[18] Sigmund Freud, 'Negation,' in *The Standard Edition of the Complete Psychological Works of Sigmund Freud*, vol. 19, ed. James Strachey (London: Hogarth Press, 1964), 236.   [19] *Ibid.*, 237.   [20] *Ibid.*, 236, 239.

become a poignant euphemism parallel to the biblical sense of 'knowing' another person; it would be an 'acquainted' like Frost's 'Acquainted With the Night,' which is at once bewilderment and epiphany, slight estrangement and total connection.

The full implications of this faculty are, as Freud sensed but barely elaborated, truly remarkable. Negation seems to suggest a vestigial ability to be two places in one identical moment and also, at the same time, at a remove from both (thus answering the Firesign Theatre question, 'How can I be two places at once, when I'm not anywhere at all?'): it explains, in short, the capacity for judgment. It is another way of articulating the possibilities implicit in Kant's *Critique of Judgement*, as it offers a model by which an external artifact – 'Beauty,' personified 'Desire' – may function outside the realm of concept as felt response, even as this nexus further promotes a discourse of judgment by which the two parties are retrieved as interdependent but somehow separate. It also holds a further knowledge of the sort that J. L. Austin articulates when he points out that in ordinary language negation is never a simple reversal – 'I love my mother' is not a mirrored reflection of 'I do not love my mother' – but instead always involves a fair degree of slippage.[21] Thrown into the balance is the acute sense that a thing once said cannot be taken back, or taken *all* back, that the fit between assertion and denial is never exact but that some performative, constative, and figurative coverage will always exist. Like some acute metaphysical conceit for completion through opposition, stasis through movement, 'negation' speaks worlds.

For one acquainted with negation – experimentally, at the level of self, and experientially, at the level of observation – this equation proves itself equally compounded of nihilism and faith, nullification and affirmation; a discourse 'not acquainted with negation' would be performing only the simulacra of judgment. It would be Schreberian in its delusion, even as it was Schreberian in its certainties and its opinions and Schreberian in its truth (which is to say that it would be absolutely true at the level of intent); it would, as did Schreber in his *Memoirs*, argue its own case with such extraordinary effectiveness that the slight matter of madness recedes into relative unimportance. Yet this assertion seems

---

[21] See J. L. Austin, 'Truth' and 'How to Talk,' in *Philosophical Papers*, ed. J. O. Urmson and G. J. Warnock (Oxford: Clarendon Press, 1990).

paradoxical or indeed counterfactual, for if the process of negation enables judgment it also reveals the external – that which may be matched up, agreed upon, used – to have been privileged at a rather high cost. Taken to its logical conclusion, a genuine familiarity with negation would bring one, not to active judgment but to watchful waiting, to the hope that some mediation between the two kinds of truth might be achieved and/or to the nihilism implied in a vision capable of entertaining two equally true truths.[22] Certainly, it would drive one from historiography toward fiction or poetry or metaphysics, and it would make language-use seem a very complicated or an utterly pragmatic proposition. And more basically even than this, such a vision would necessitate a reinvention of the concept of 'history,' as it would take one out of the game as it has been traditionally played; engaging in what some feminist philosophers have called a 'maternal ethic' of watchfulness and an abeyance of the punitive or the pre-emptive would obviate the possibility of enacting large, 'history-making' gestures. To judge, as *Senatspräsident* Schreber would tell one, is to take the terrifying responsibility of being definitive; one cannot do it, either for a living or in any way that seriously effects the lives of others, who is besieged by alternative versions of truth. There must be some mechanism to arrest this process midway in order for work to get done or history to get told. And *voilà*, here is Oedipus to save the day.

Again, there is an odor of necessity, as if Oedipus wanders toward Freud because he is fated to meet up with him, to solve this new riddle in advance – indeed, to allow it to be *heard* in the first place – and to best once and for all that enigmatic bundle of negation (figural, psychic, and formal), the female sphinx. For only with an Oedipal system in place is one allowed full recognition of what it means to spare the rod and spoil the child. In this elegant tautology one sees that without a castration fantasy to license this insight into negation, the implications for any man who aspires to a place in history would be terrifying: without Oedipal pedagogy to privilege an external, socialized reality over the other, one would suffer the alternative emasculation of what would appear from the outside as 'passivity,' which is to say, watchfulness, reticence, and careful, genuine negotiation. How utterly different

[22] See Iris Murdoch, *The Sovereignty of Good* (London: Ark, 1985).

'history' would become, without its great men, its wars, its grand rises and cataclysmic falls and inexorable declines, for without the curious paradox of judgment as we have come to know it all gestures would be minimalist, smaller, more diffident; the sense of which Lyotard speaks of being part of the referent, history, would overcome the fantasy of detachment. The differences between history and autobiography and novel-writing would diminish to almost nothing, as one could only speak locally, and only with full recognition of his own intimate and personal stake in the utterances that emerged. This would be catastrophic, for speaking personally is, as everyone knows, a female habit; what stands as methodological rigor as regards historical evidence in a system committed to 'objectivity' might be called something less noble – gossip, for example – if it were taken to have been gathered as much for personal pleasure, predisposition, or necessity as for the public good.

Barthes' assertion that objective history-writers and schizophrenics are not acquainted with negation is, then, multiply provocative as regards acts of judgment in general and historiographic judgment in particular. I would revise Barthes' formulation, however, for if schizophrenics are in fact incapable of negation – and they may well be – it is precisely the historian's acquaintance with the phenomenon that ensures his stalwart rejection of its complexities for the more decisively unilateral gestures of manliness. With Schreber in mind, one can return to the question of stress within historical discourse, for Schreber has been postulated as a model of acute Oedipal anxiety, and as the embodiment of one pushed by this anxiety into an impeccable system of logic, productive of hermeneutically true and convincing judgments that are nonetheless felt juridically, medically, and socially as 'mad.' By Freud's reading, 'Schreber' is a text where Oedipal strictures have dismantled the capacity for negation: Schreber-text tells all the truth and tells it straight, not slant, and thus he is read as the best and most reliable historian of himself as he translates the past into the present through his *Memoirs.* Judge Schreber is the terrifying specter of what it means to fall on the wrong side of the Oedipal fence, into a fully activated amnesia about alternative possibilities for truth. One must, in the Oedipal balancing act, be neither too cognizant of alternative possibilities nor too distracted from them, else 'history' goes underground.

One could say, then, without fully subscribing to Barthes' formulation, that conventional historiography is more than ordinarily fraught, that its own assumptions, its own shouldering of conflictual responsibilities, its own self-articulated anxiety of influence push it toward Oedipal overcompensation. Paradoxically, one of the clues to this stress may be found in the antagonism toward psychohistory of historiography proper, which manifests a curiously chilling attitude toward an enterprise which by all rights it should see as congenial to its interests. It is as if historiography's stake in Oedipal amnesia is so high that it cannot bear the specific discourse by which this dynamic is brought fully to light.

Psychohistory and historiography

If between the historians and the psychohistorians there is something less than cordial relations, if the historians charge the psychohistorians with infiltrating good, plain narrative with a foreign host, the hostilities derive from the contestation of common ground. As if often the case in such disputes, their working premises are quite similar, their methodological assumptions congenial if not identical, their predisposition toward non-technical language shared; yet the historians and the psychohistorians nonetheless find bones to pick. And indeed, as non-psychoanalytically inclined historians, among others, have pointed out, 'Psychoanalysis' enforces its own peculiarly invasive linguistic and conceptual systems and can, in fact, generate a virtually Schreberian paranoia as regards its consumptive power. (And as with Schreber, 'paranoia' is not precisely the most accurate term, for it is true that even those who claim to be free of psychoanalytic influence can be said by Freudian initiates to be implicated as they speak in ways that may always be translated back toward the holy source, proof positive, in this theocratic and utterly circular reasoning, of the Truth making itself manifest even among the heathens.) By its enemies psychoanalysis is perceived as insidious, imperialistic, and opportunistic. Gertrude Himmelfarb begins her essay, 'Case Studies in Psychohistory,' with: 'The critic of psychohistory is at some peril. His motives can be impugned, his criticisms can be 'psychoanalyzed away,' A panoply of psychoanalytic concepts can be invoked to explain his obtuseness: denial, repression, resistance, evasion, anxiety, rage.'[23] As Gay points out, one of the standard indictments is that psychoanalysis explains everything and therefore nothing, that it is (maddeningly) irrefutable and smugly impervious precisely because it is felt by initiates as a revealed truth. 'A theory which is not refutable by any conceivable event is non-scientific,' says Popper. 'Irrefutability is not a virtue of a theory . . . but a vice': psychoanalysis, by this standard reading, is a theology posing as a science.[24] The Gordian knot becomes a complex tangle of snakes in this view, and the sword does little good in slicing through a system in which a sword will never be only a sword, never mind the snakes. One may walk away, but to stay in striking range is to get bitten. When Barzun speaks bitterly of the 'weazel words' spawned within psychohistorical assessments of character, whereby 'Language does the work of suborning the witness,' his image communicates this sense of a language, ruthless, relentless, vicious, and slippery; it is impossible not to feel Barzun's extremism as speaking to a metatextual fear as well, that the historian-witness will also be suborned if he opens his language to include the contradictions inherent in negational thinking. In Barzun's view psychoanalysis does not, in fact it *cannot*, respect the boundaries between a language of facts and a language of inference, and between 'ascertained particulars and inductive generalities,' and it is thus inevitably contaminative as it is allowed to enter historiographic work.[25] Psychoanalysis is, as Barzun's rhetoric makes clear, felt to be an unmanly weapon, operating by innuendo and sly implicature to distract language from its obligation to straightforward communicative clarity.

If, by its opponents it is felt as opportunistic and insidious, by its advocates psychoanalysis is authorized as necessarily penetrative and encompassing; it is organic, protean, capable of subtle adjustments, systematically adaptive. It – Psychoanalysis – is a body like the analyst's body in that it remembers the past, learns from experience, alters through time, and responds to the particularities at hand; it values memory, seeks to reclaim lost evidence and bring it into narrative, and works to cultivate territories lost to disorder and to the subterfuges of the unconscious. By this view, the

[23] Gertrude Himmelfarb, *The New History and the Old: Critical Essays and Reappraisals* (Cambridge: Harvard University Press, 1987), 107.
[24] Peter Gay, *Freud for Historians* (New York: Oxford University Press, 1985), 62–64.
[25] Barzun, *Clio and the Doctors*, 44–45.

psychoanalyst is in some very pertinent sense a quintessential historian, bringing to fruition the historian's long commitment to an informed evaluation of human behaviour. In one thing the two sides generally agree, and that is to acknowledge that psychoanalysis has formidable power as a language system whose terms, authorized by their affiliation (or quasi-affiliation) with science, physiology, neurology, clinical observation, and methodological self-consciousness, stand as powerfully mediative within a larger system of concepts regarding human nature. It would be a mere truism to say that psychoanalysis reclothes the insights of art; Harold Bloom has, he says, argued for years that Freud is 'prosified Shakespeare,' his 'vision of human psychology . . . derived, not altogether unconsciously, from his reading of Shakespeare's plays.'[26] But it does not hurt to recall Freud's insistent return to literary texts and his claim in 'Those Wrecked by Success' that the analysis of character, fictional and real, may take place within a loop in which validation of insights is reciprocal.[27] His considerable power as a reader of texts affords a means of enforcing the potency of his own evaluative system: if psychoanalytic assumptions enjoy a Rosetta stone status, providing explanations that work retroactively to bring all literature into a single comprehensible humanism, one might logically assume that this is a status accorded to the finally revealed truth. Under this positivist reading, one sees Freud's work as both powerfully synthetic, gathering up the loose, 'poetic' versions of human nature as a scientist gathers data and turning them into usable terms within a dependable system of analysis, and as thoroughly inventive.

The alternative argument – that the literary texts themselves, in a very specific way, provoke the psychoanalytic system which glosses them – redistributes causality but does not otherwise challenge the potency of the psychoanalytic insights those texts inspire. One might very well argue what I believe to be the case: that an insightful reader who comes to speak and to write of texts tends to reproduce the terms of the texts upon which s/he comments, and this not merely at a general level but at the level of

[26] Harold Bloom, 'Freud: A Shakespearean Reading,' *Yale Review*, 82, 3 (July 1994), 1.

[27] Sigmund Freud, 'Some Character-Types Met With in Psychoanalytic Work' (1925), in *The Standard Edition of the Complete Psychological Works*, ed. James Strachey (London: Hogarth Press, 1964), 331.

individual words, tropological systems, and image patterns. In this reading, the meta-textual language of psychoanalysis comes secondarily from Freud's clinical experience and primarily from his literary ones (which is not to devalue the insights or to impugn his clinical acuity but merely to suggest an impetus originally more linguistically material than materially linguistic). In other words, one could premise that the psychoanalytic system whose language translates an entire history of literature into itself is able to do so because it is, in fact, that literature which has initialized the discourse at a highly specific semantic and linguistic level. Bloom says, 'Shakespeare haunted Freud as he haunts the rest of us: deliberately and unintentionally, Freud found himself quoting (and misquoting) Shakespeare in conversation, in his letters, and in the writings which created for psychoanalysis a literature of its own';[28] one might go a step further and claim as formative all those poetic texts whose holistic versions of the human condition exude themselves at every level from the lyrical to the prosaic. Shakespeare is perhaps only the sufficient and necessary metonymy for a body of work whose semantic, rhythmic, tropological, imagistic, and symbolic fields generate repetition of themselves within a meta-textual environment whose subject is humanness and, as well, generate a correlative language of explanation and exegesis. But however the influence may be assigned, whether literature in all its extraordinary richness provokes psychoanalysis into being as one more critical meta-text among many or whether psychoanalysis both explains the inchoate voice of literature and in the process *creates* a new version of humanness, psychoanalysis has a condensed, virtually inexorable power.

Thus, if one side among the historians sees psychoanalytic power as fully legitimate, which is as much as to say, obliquely or directly, that those who resist psychoanalysis most nearly prove by their resistance its universal applicability, the other side does not see it as powerless but as holding a ruthlessly imperialistic power without legitimacy and, given the apparent adequacy of less technical models of explanation, without benefit. And indeed, psychoanalysis can be a stern paternal taskmaster for those who embrace it, so much so that devotees from other fields occasionally feel themselves in the erotically charged but degraded position of

---

[28] Bloom, 'Freud,' 1.

supplicant to deity, slave to master, female to male, feminine to masculine, (Schreber) son to (Schreber) father; if Schreber feels himself invaded by rays, if he is at risk of violation every time he allows his mind to go empty for a moment, he is the hyperbole by which such discursive infiltrations as are enacted by psychoanalysis may be recognized. As Meltzer says, 'psychoanalysis becomes a ubiquitous subject, assimilating every object into itself. But it is also a Subject which sees itself as omnipresent, omniscient, and without a center – precisely the terms in which God has been described. It is not then by chance that the unconscious is likened to a divinity; always present but revealing itself only obliquely and at privileged moments, the unconscious takes the place of the Judeo-Christian God. It is within every being, but inaccessible unless it 'chooses' to manifest itself.'[29]

Psychoanalysis has a liquid capacity to permeate, to soak through several layers (this assumption of permeability is, after all, descriptive of its rationale and its methodology), so that its effect is felt at the level of text and metatext, and at the level of object text and critical text. It is also constructive, in that it systematizes discrete informational details – the stuff of which history is made – into a formal mode whose structural integrity is inextricable from its analytic soundness (Freud's models change but the topological energy of the enterprise is stable); Barzun is not alone among the enemies of psychohistory in his translation of this formative power into a unilateral determinism. Moreover, western and westernized discourse is suffused with the terms of psychoanalysis, both because many of these terms were taken from common usage and given technical status and because many of them have reverted to generalized or metaphorical use[30]; there is an ongoing reciprocity between psychoanalytic and ordinary language in which dissemination is purchased at what is said to be the small expense of technical precision – the patristic mode yields to the less containable operations of the layman.

This destabilizing of terms is more necessarily the case in an historiographic situation which rejects because of its traditional commitment to ordinary language the constant, thorough deploy-

---

[29] Françoise Meltzer, in *The Trials of Psychoanalysis*, ed. Françoise Meltzer (University of Chicago Press, 1988), 2.

[30] See Laplanche, *Life and Death in Psychoanalysis*, on the word 'ego' as it is used in Freud's text both as metaphor and as metonymy.

ment of a *specific*, technically precise analytic language within its narrative structure. This colloquializing is felt by opponents as making psychohistory both less succinctly psychoanalytic and more invasive, 'weazly,' as Barzun would have it. Without apparent irony, Barzun sets up the mutually exclusive terms by which psychohistoriography must abide: it must be untechnical but absolutely precise in its deployment of the technical. 'In history proper,' says Barzun, 'the presence of untechnical language, the absence of jargon, are required.' But in psychohistory, he says, 'the vocabulary defeats its own ends. The reason is not that the words are unfamiliar, but that they are disparate and used without strictness. In short, the matter of history has been subordinated to a specialism which on reflection does not sustain its claim.'[31] And yet, one senses the real anxiety in this strange logic, as it seems to imagine a potent psychoanalysis set loose, in disguise, dressed like ordinary people. Like Hawthorne's allegorizing of Transcendentalism as an amorphous but powerful mist towering above, in this fantasy Psychoanalysis assumes huge dimensions which lose their definitive shape even as the concepts themselves may gain in totemic power.

Obliquely, paradoxically, but most powerfully, psychoanalysis also resects the Cartesian mind/body split by creating a version of humanness that is at once all body and nobody; it contains all the provisions for an historical subject in time and, by virtue of having become history, above time. If, as Meltzer says, the unconscious has the power of divinity, it is a divinity entailed by humanness and deriving its potency from a confluence of visceral and cerebral energies; as with Donne's compass, its two parts may be felt to lean all the more toward each other as the distance between them widens. Authorized by an Aristotelian taxonomy of physics/metaphysics and susceptible therefore always to the diametrically opposed charges of metaphysical bias and pansexualism, psychoanalysis may also reawaken a dream of unification; and if this dream is always incomplete or cracked because the body–mind is damaged, it is nonetheless a holistic deterioration. On Freud's authority, Lacan hypostasizes this power in the Phallus, the term most perfectly suited to communicate a Hoffmanesque vision of intellectual sensuality, winged and transcen-

[31] Barzun, *Clio and the Doctors*, 16–17.

dent. Lacan's terms are almost paradoxically theistic, God cloaked in a prophylactic of mystery: 'The position of the phallus is always veiled. It appears only in sudden manifestations [*dans des phanies*], in a flash, by means of its reflection on the level of the object. For the subject, of course, it is a question of to have it or not to have it. But the radical position of the subject at the level of privation, of the subject as subject of desire, is not to be it. The subject is himself, so to speak, a negative object.'[32] *Anti-Oedipus* puts the Lacanian case more generally: 'This lack with something in common, the great Phallus, the Lack with two nonsuperimposable sides, is purely mythical; it is like the One in negative theology, it introduces lack into desire and causes exclusive series to emanate, to which it attributes a goal, an origin, and a path of resignation.'[33] All body and nobody, desire and privation; psychoanalysis is a humanism, a metalanguage structured so as to assimilate all terms, past and present, into itself. It may be felt as outside of time by those susceptible to its power, for it works retroactively and into the future to claim meaning for itself.

Yet all of these warnings aside and without acceding to the psychoanalytic gambit which would use the historian's resistance to analytic assumptions as proof of their applicability, one can argue that historiography and psychoanalysis are well matched, both at the level of process and of product, and that it is this very compatibility that increases the threat that psychoanalysis will encroach on historical procedures by revealing the necessity by which oedipalized judgment is formed. Collingwood, speaking ironically, even, one feels, paradoxically, makes a deadly accurate assessment when he says that the psychologist 'might for example argue that historians are people who build up a fantasy-world, like artists, because they are too neurotic to live effectively in the world, but, unlike artists, project this fantasy-world into the past because they connect the origin of their neuroses with past events in their own childhood and always go back and back to the past in a vain attempt to disentangle these neuroses. This analysis might go into further detail, and show how the historian's interest in a

[32] Jacques Lacan, 'Desire and the Interpretation of Desire in *Hamlet*,' in *Literature and Psychoanalysis: The Question of Reading: Otherwise*, Yale French Studies, 55–56 (1977), 48–49.

[33] Gilles Deleuze and Felix Guattari, *Anti-Oedipus: Capitalism and Schizophrenia*, trans. Robert Hurley, Mark Seem, and Helen R. Lane (Minneapolis: University of Minnesota Press, 1989), 59–60.

commanding figure such as Julius Caesar expresses his childish attitude to his father, and so on.'[34]

As Langer and others have said, the historian from Thucydides on has claimed a psychologist's insightfulness regarding human behaviors;[35] he has the watchful habits and the documentary instincts of the clinician coupled with the advantage of an entire history of case histories. The compatibilities between history and psychoanalysis increase the stakes both for those historians who subscribe to psychohistoriographic methods and those who reject them, for the already potent discourse of psychoanalysis flourishes (like weeds or flowers, depending on the view) within a discipline whose members are intent upon being a guild of productive men who build on solid ground, who resist the seductions of the various pathologies they document historically. Historiography's preoccupation with normalcy at the level of text production – that is to say, 'normal' narrative constructions, neither chronologically nor tropologically elaborate, neither technically nor theoretically inaccessible – mirrors psychoanalysis's interest in normalizing analysands in ways that will mobilize them sufficiently in the world of work and human relationships; whether or not there is some covert or overt affiliation with less mainstream impulses, the tradition analyst and the historian feel themselves ethically bound to communicate *at the level of practice and of performance* the value of integration.

Where another discipline might work to speak of normalcy and pathology while, in so speaking, itself enacting a discourse in some way 'extremist' (lyrical, highly figurative, highly theoretical, structurally complex, etc.), historiography aspires to *be* normal and thus always runs the Schreberian risk of being driven away from this normalcy toward the messianic. Put in terms of the classic dismissal of literary realism as being by its very nature ideologically compromised, historiography's affiliation with plain narrative enforces normalcy regardless of the subject about which the narrative speaks. It would seek explanations for failures personal and political not as explanation only but as potential amelioration: this is an obligation perceived to necessitate reason-

[34] R. J. Collingwood, *The Idea of History*, ed. Jan Van Der Dussen (Oxford: Clarendon Press, 1993), 2.

[35] William L. Langer, 'The Next Assignment,' *American Historical Review*, 63, 2 (January 1958), 285.

ableness both at the level of analysis and of exegesis, even if there is sympathy with or admiration for the individuality which resists full assimilation into larger systems. 'Historical men' are men whose subjectivist preoccupations are meaningful precisely in the ways that these preoccupations intersect with action in the world (that which is historically documentable); as Hegel says in *Lectures on the Philosophy of History*, family and personal matters may produce narratives, 'But it is only the state which first presents subject-matter that is not only *adapted* to the prose of History, but involves the production of such history in the very progress of its own being.'[36]

And, because history *must* concern itself with a detailing that is essentially chronotopic, historians may document pathology but cannot valorize the idiosyncratic, the non-reproduceable, the lyrical, the mad, or the eccentric by reproducing their effects textually. The chronotopic mode which explicates space through references to temporality and time through spatial images can communicate the strange and disjunctive when one uses it, as for instance Woolf does in *Mrs. Dalloway* or Faulkner does in *As I Lay Dying*, to suggest a simultaneity of competing realities within the same historical space, or to subvert the 'real' and the 'sane' by implicitly linking it with madness. But when chronology is sacrosanct and the 'real' – the historical real of things, peoples, economies, and wars – is one's main concern, then chronotopic language only cements normalcy in place. The historiographic insistence upon plain language is a value system as well as a mode of communication, a system whose moral obligations are those of the good citizen: to be 'objective' rather than idiosyncratic, to be serious rather than whimsical or flippant or frivolous, to be 'realistic' rather than foolishly idealistic or flamboyantly imaginative. And, in *being* these things at the performative level of the text, to encourage their growth in others. The precedent is at least as old as Aristotle, who argued that political speech should resist temptations to ornament itself; serious matters deserve 'clear and appropriate language: any more elaborateness would involve distortions introduced to sway what must be a debased audience.'[37] The historian who is guilty of too selfish a preoccupation –

---

[36] Quoted in Hayden White, *The Content of the Form: Narrative Discourse and Historical Representation* (Baltimore: Johns Hopkins University Press, 1987), 12.
[37] Kittay and Godzich, *The Emergence of Prose*, 189.

with style, with persuasion, with the pleasures of language – does wrong by his craft, not just at the level of disciplinary decorum but at the moral level as well.

Loewenberg's choice of Freud's 'Those Wrecked by Success' as the text most central to discussions of historical figures communicates this information at two levels: at the level of narrative, it suggests that the standard rise and fall pattern of men and nations is due to the resurgence of imperatives from an interior indifferent to socialized concerns; but at a metatextual level Freud's text stands as well as warning – the historian is not meant merely to give object lessons but to take them as well, and the successful historian will fall if, in his success, he yields to anarchic demands felt as subjectivism. (This, one will remember, is Gay's reading in *Freud for Historians* of how historians come to write *about* historiography only to conclude that 'subjectivism' is a sad inevitability about which one must write objectively and with care.) Historiography proper shares with psychohistoriography this need to *be* as well as to tell about a normalcy that will allow for productive work in the world; its narrative habits, so congenial with nineteenth-century novels of realism, share realism's concern to put aside anarchic pleasure for productivity, just as they share realism's inevitable and always more or less uneasy intuition that such language makes its own pleasures, whether one will or no. And in this venue, psychoanalysis takes on formidable dimensions for its enemies as well as its advocates, as it formalizes historiography's impulse to explain pathology and to eschew it at the same time even as it lays bare the very root of the problem. Freud must take literally the possibility that to talk about sex, no matter how necessary, is to *be* sexy, and in a defensive move says, as a preliminary to his discussion of Dora, 'I will simply claim for myself the rights of the gynaecologist – or rather much more modest ones – and add that it would be the mark of a singular and perverse prurience to suppose that conversations of this kind are a good means of exciting or of gratifying sexual desires.'[38] Historiography, with a similar case-history obligation to the physical and material details of humanness, must defend against its own appetitive effects: it must walk that straight and narrow line in which narrative language promotes moderation – normalcy – over

---

[38] Sigmund Freud, *Dora: An Analysis of a Case of Hysteria* (New York: Collier, 1963), 22–23.

desire even as it is committed to the sexy tangibilities of the circumstantial.

The marriage of history and psychoanalysis may be said to have been made in heaven, for both may be read as a locating of physics within metaphysics, yet with the rather heroic determination to give the physical, the circumstantial, and the diurnal its full due. Freud's atheism is a red herring and his physiological determinisms so equivocal as to yield always to the complex indeterminacies of what one is tempted to call 'spirit,' and yet he keeps the body *here*, before our eyes and sensually apparent. Freud is, says Deleuze, as prophetically inclined as Jung, for the mythic structure that upholds psychoanalytic order is systemically permeated with the gods; and 'to render religion unconscious, or the unconscious religious, still amounts to injecting something religious into the unconscious.'[39] But if the material and circumstantial predispositions in psychoanalysis may be felt to disguise an essential idealism, psychoanalysis nonetheless, as does history, gives the devil its due by returning again and again to a vision more visceral than spiritual. Yet if the effort at resection is commendable, the problems are apparently insuperable, for there are multiple concentricities of resistance against stabilizing a holistic body–mind. Each separate system is internally fraught, and independent systems are thrown into competing relationships with each other. The relationship between psychoanalysis and psychohistory is one such dynamic, whereby the former becomes the meta-text by which the latter is controlled and through which it is demoted to the place of physicalities and temporalities; the relationship between metaphysics and history is similarly deployed, and the permutations continue, with history erecting itself above psychohistory, and so on. And whatever it may have originally been, the Oedipal narrative becomes successively, multiply overdetermined within a closed system that equilibrates itself relentlessly; so enriched, it must necessarily come to seem an essentialism. Abnegation of desire, transcendence into an asymptotic relationship with wisdom: the Oedipal story, via Freud, is the parable from which and into which this system proceeds.

The process of such story-telling, once begun, is determined by a certain limited number of textual markers, under whose impera-

---

[39] *Anti-Oedipus*, 58.

tives one sees or fails to see the available evidence: because narrative is itself fraught with a long and dense history, one is, as story-teller, under compulsions and secret directives relative to outcome that are strangely similar to the dilemma Oedipus himself embodies; the attempt to wrest narrative from overt and clandestine inevitabilities is accompanied always by a sense that language is having its own secret way. As Nietzsche says, 'all concepts in which an entire process is semiotically concentrated elude definition; only that which has no history is definable.'[40] To put it in Freudian terms, the story-teller who elects to stay within realism's province (as opposed to modernist experimentations or the more radical resistance to linearity embodied in avant gardism) must necessarily repress this knowledge of an archeological density in order to produce a more syntagmatic, product-driven narrative. He is to speak a story whose standards have long been set and whose terms have come to seem congenital, but he is to make it powerful and true to the maxim that 'Human actions – or inactions – depend on a rich mixture of motives.'[41] It is, then, no wonder that this intuition seeps continually through in the reiterated form of that most anxiety-driven of stories: the *Oedipus*.

Historiographical text production both invites and exploits Oedipus' willingness to show up, combat ready for the task of shouldering other men off the road; its narrative equilibrations – between fact and the fictional mode in which they are presented, between analytic, statistical, or technical language and ordinary language, between Truth and truth, etc. – virtually guarantee the litanic repetition either of Oedipal terms explicitly displayed or of an oedipalized structure: if not the Oedipal story as narrative, then the Oedipal story *in* narrative, at the level of procedure, expectations, negotiation (this is an insight explored thematically and structurally in Kundera's *The Unbearable Lightness of Being*, as *Oedipus* becomes, as the drama unfolds, a dominant political motif played off against the aesthetic anxiety condensed in his ruminations on *Kitsch*). For oedipalized narrative is by its nature a solution to the competing imperatives between autonomy and authority, the particular and the universal, the personal and the politicized. It is the archetype for a pragmatic forgetfulness which

---

[40] Friedrich Nietzsche, *On the Genealogy of Morals*, trans. ed. Walter Kaufmann (New York: Vintage, 1969), 80.
[41] Barzun, *Clio and the Doctors*, 44.

leaves to fate the impossible contradictions upon which the exegetical structure rests, and as far as language is concerned it is the very source from which the technicalities of psychoanalysis come and back to which historiography insists, in its rejection of analytic terminology, that they recede. Ironically, it is also original proof for the historian's claim that psychohistory is a redundant term, an unnecessary encumbrance in jargon of the historian's own well-cultivated psychological insights. And whatever else must be forgotten in the process of falling into the old Oedipal habit, it is a hedge against loss of control – i.e., feminization, Clio on the prowl: the wisdom of the fathers is as much an acquisitive amnesia regarding spiritual, erotic, and intellectual distractions as it is an assimilation of those cultural memories most suited to progenitive success.

'Daddy,' says Sylvia Plath, 'I have had to kill you . . . / Marble-heavy, a bag full of God.' As Plath's poem makes more than painfully clear (and Plath backs her assertion with the unequivocal gesture of suicide, the end of history), it is the quintessence of the Oedipal to be a warning that you will be damned if you do, damned if you don't. Virile moderation, a manly Aristotelian balance between desire and control, paternal murder phantasmatically translated into socially, economically, militaristically, politically productive metaphors of itself: these are the only terms of reconciliation imaginable within the bloody extremisms of the Oedipal dilemma. Plath's 'Daddy,' read with Aristotelian eyes, is an obscene poem because it does not merely express a wish to kill the father, but enacts that killing by revealing his power as ugly, Hitleresque, sado-masochistic. Because it is also the ultimate form of negation, where 'I kill you' means 'I bring you back to life' and where 'I hate you' means 'I love you,' it becomes as unsettling a performance of the double truth of the Oedipal contract as one could ever find.

> I have always been scared of *you*,
> With your Luftwaffe, your gobbledygoo.
> And your neat moustache
> And your Aryan eye, bright blue,
> Panzer-man, panzer-man, O You–
>
> Not God but a swastika
> So black no sky could squeak through.

> Every woman adores a Fascist,
> The boot in the face, the brute
> Brute heart of a brute like you.

This poem does not merely articulate but it re-enacts the full Sophoclean tragedy, and as such it stands as an antithesis to the successfully oedipalized narratives through which history must make itself known. A liberation from filial diffidence and from the decorous mock-killings of balanced discourse, it is also a most effective warning. Its intuition of the father as revenant is a precise trope for Oedipal symbiosis, for the father must, in the Oedipal bargain, be counted among the undead and he must, in his power, bring the sons into the charmed circle of Oedipal myopia, where one can be simultaneously two places at once and not anywhere at all. *Agon* rather than agony ('I like a look of Agony,' says Dickinson, 'Because I know it's true'). Plath does the unthinkable and ends the cycle:

> If I've killed one man, I've killed two –
> The vampire who said he was you
> And drank my blood for a year,
> Seven years, if you want to know.
> Daddy, you can lie back now.
>
> There's a stake in your fat black heart
> And the villagers never liked you.
> They are dancing and stamping on you.
> They always *knew* it was you.
> Daddy, daddy, you bastard, I'm through.

Plath shares Schreber's intuition that the Oedipal negotiation forces one into a double indemnity whose weight may be felt as 'soul murder'; it is no wonder that conventional historiography shoulders the burden of normalcy, and that it feels bound to fight for reasonableness and moderation, to discover 'truth' of a particular, manly kind and to perform the methodological rituals of evidence which function as purifications and obeisances. One bound to such difficult restitution either succeeds and becomes a man, or fails and becomes, like Schreber, a madman whose synonymity is to 'woman.' Either side of the balance failing, productivity might turn to carnage or impotence, language might turn to poetry, bellowing, or unapologetic fiction or fall into silence. History's nightmares, in fact.

3

Daddy: notes upon an autobiographical account of paranoia

Thus in the case of Schreber we find ourselves once again upon the familiar ground of the father-complex.
'Psychoanalytic Notes Upon an Autobiographical Account of a Case of Paranoia (Dementia Paranoides)'

> You stand at the blackboard, daddy,
> In the picture I have of you,
> A cleft in your chin instead of your foot
> But no less a devil for that, no not
> And less the black man who
>
> Bit my pretty red heart in two.
> I was ten when they buried you.
> At twenty I tried to die
> And get back, back, back to you.
> I thought even the bones would do.
>
> But they pulled me out of the sack,
> And they stuck me together with glue.
> And then I knew what to do.
> I made a model of you,
> A man in black with a Meinkampf look
>
> And a love of the rack and screw.
> And I said I do, I do.
> > Sylvia Plath, 'Daddy'

The Schreber case

With the publication in 1959 of William Niederland's paper, 'Schreber: Father and Son,' the case of Daniel Paul Schreber, presented at length by Schreber himself in his 1903 *Memoirs of My Nervous Illness*, became irrevocably intertwined with the story of

Schreber's father, Dr. Daniel Gottlieb Moritz Schreber.[1] Its unusual textual status already challenging the boundaries of various genres and disciplines, the Schreber case after this moment in 1959 awakened the need for and increasing inevitability of further historical and biographical research. The pursuit of biographical details pertaining both to the son and the father has since created an Oedipal industry whose product reciprocates the energies behind its production and whose form negotiates a territory between case-history, history, biography, and psychobiography.[2] The two figures of son and father now stand opposed and yet inseparable, their stature allegorical in proportion and effect. Paradoxically, the historical and biographical detailing that has followed upon Niederland's thesis, because it has been deployed in the service of the Oedipal story, has not softened the iconographic dimensions of this pairing: the mythic proportions, far from diminishing under the effects of rival theories and circumstantialities, are sustained by the elaborations of the various cults of Oedipus. Freud's original reading of Schreber as a man locked in a deadly Oedipal struggle has been clinched in a series of studies whose own engagements with the Father of Psychoanalysis and his surrogates replay the very Oedipal game they have come to referee. By bringing to trial the father Freud ignored, they are able at once to confirm his Oedipal reading and go him one better; their oedipalized energy is not, thus, amenable to articulations that might fall outside of this power struggle. Spiritually, psychically, and textually hyperbolic in itself, the Schreber story in

[1] William Niederland, 'Schreber: Father and Son,' *Psychoanalytic Quarterly*, 28, 4 (October 1959); reprinted, 'slightly amended,' in William G. Niederland, M.D., *The Schreber Case: Psychoanalytic Profile of a Paranoid Personality* (New York: Quadrangle, 1974), 49–62.

[2] The four main texts under consideration here will be Niederland's book-length study, *The Schreber Case*, Morton Schatzman's *Soul Murder: Persecution in the Family* (New York: Random House, 1973); Han Israels' *Schreber: Father and Son* (Madison, Conn.: International Universities Press, Inc., 1989); and Zvi Lothane's *In Defense of Schreber: Soul Murder and Psychiatry* (Hillsdale, N.J.: Analytic Press, 1992). A highly abbreviated list of work on psychohistoriography would include: Geoffrey Cocks and Travis l. Crosby, eds., *Psycho/History: Readings in the Method of Psychology, Psychoanalysis, and History* (New Haven: Yale University Press, 1987); Saul Friedlander, *History and Psychoanalysis: An Inquiry into the Possibilities and Limits of Psychohistory*, trans. Susan Suleiman (New York: Holmes and Meier Publishers, Inc., 1978); William McKinley Runyan, *Life Histories and Psychobiography: Explorations in Theory and Method* (New York: Oxford University Press, 1982); and Runyan, ed. *Psychology and Historical Interpretation* (New York: Oxford University Press, 1988).

both its primary and secondary forms may be taken as emblematic. As it writes large the teleological assumptions which more usually remain tacit in the historiographical process, the Schreber case may be felt to expose the complex fate of traditionally defined historiography: to be on a road rich with unexpected detail and filled with surprises, while at the same time bound within a narrative whose conclusions have been written in advance.

Niederland's thesis, that Schreber's illness could be traced directly and specifically to the father through ample textual evidence, created, in effect, an additional set of imperatives regarding discussions of the etiology of paranoia in general and of the etiology of Schreber's paranoia in particular (Schatzman, for example, extrapolates from Moritz Schreber the idea of 'paranoidogenicity,' a condition associated with the person 'who *gen*erates paranoid states in others'), but it also served to confirm and throw into strong relief Freud's most basic assumptions.[3] Niederland's evidence of paternal abuse acted as a lever that shifted the entire narrative structure regarding Schreber onto a parallel track; and by obviating the possibility of isolating Schreber's psychopathology from detailed considerations of his contextual and historical past relative to his father, it intimated, with the force of a strong caricature, that psychobiography's Oedipal procedures were legitimate. Moritz Schreber's theories regarding childrearing, his overarching imposition of a rigorous hygienics, his pedagogic and disciplinary relentlessness, and his use of material devices designed either as orthopedic or as prophylactic have so compellingly been linked to the self-articulated terms of Schreber's delusions that any consideration of the relatively stark outlines of Freud's initial analysis will now inevitably be conducted within an enriched discursive field. Freud locates Schreber's pathology in his immediate history, that is to say, within the space between biological and psychic determinisms whose shorthand is 'Oedipus,' and as he considers the universalities from which one branches off into paranoia or neuroses or relative normalcy he obviates the necessity for any detailed consideration of the particular father, and the particular history extending backwards into time (his much-quoted admission that one could wish for evidence beyond his own relatively

[3] See Schatzman, *Soul Murder*, 137–38.

circumscribed engagement in the case is contravened by his authoritative procedures). Niederland, and those writing after him, open the case and extend it backwards, and yet the more things change the more they stay the same. Under the Oedipal spell, their use of obviously relevant but multi-dimensional texts, including the wondrous world of Schreber's delusional system, is delimited before the fact into a recapitulation, in both form and content, of the Oedipal line.

We have in Schreber's story an unprecedented situation relative to the kinds of evidence considered as crucial for psychobiographical and historiographical assessments: the son has written a long and detailed account of his nervous illness from within the stated conviction that his account is accurate, relatively sane, and, though in part visionary, nonetheless prophetically and literally true; the attending physician, Weber, has documented and re-documented his findings in testimony designed to be persuasive in a court of law; the court itself has documented its ruling and the precise terms of its decision; the father who is implicated by virtue of his treatment of the son has documented his childrearing practices at length in multiple texts, and he has, moreover, left diagrammatic evidence of the physical extensions of his theoretical assumptions. He has, by his own written account, conducted his familial duties according to the principles he outlines in his books, and this is a claim that may be to some extent directly verified by witnesses other than Daniel Paul Schreber. We have, in other words, a complete set of relevant texts whose various affiliations – with pedagogy, with legal testimony, with medical case history, with prophecy – suggest that the parties involved wrote with something like honest conviction and sincerity (this is different from saying that these texts are 'true' or transparent or rhetorically unbiased).

The *Memoirs* are and have from the beginning been felt as irresistibly authentic, with a kind of mad pathos of truthfulness. As Israels points out, almost immediately after its publication, Schreber's book was reviewed in various psychiatric journals, whose respondents anticipate Freud's assessment of the evidential validity of the text. Israels quotes Hans Schultze (1905), who writes, 'Anyone who takes an interest in the psychology of paranoiacs is recommended to read this book, which provides us with an account of the origin and development of a highly complex delusional system such as we are rarely given by our patients.'[4] It is worth noting that there is an Alice-in-Wonderland strangeness in writing a 'review' of a text apprehended as a metonymous extension of the body-mind that writes it. The review is a very specific genre that necessarily accords intentionality, control, and the possibility of authority to the writer under consideration; if it measures success (at least in some genres) in proportion to the author's capacity to offer a seamless joining of craftmanship and 'authenticity,' it presumes that this realness gains its value in competition with the artificial constraints of form. Only inasmuch as lyricism exists as in tension with its own rationality and will is it felt to have become something other than infantile or insane. But Schreber's text is apprehended as an *embodiment* of madness whose authority preempts all other considerations. It is felt as the lyric poem is felt, and while one might wonder if a less prepossessing text – a less aesthetically pleasing effort – would enjoy, and suffer, the same authority, this skepticism yields to the power of Schreber's story.

Moreover, from the point of view of historiographic procedure, we have a series of overlapping accounts which allows for the testing of individual evidence against concurrent evaluations. We have what the psychohistorian dreams of finding – hard textual evidence, complete with illustrations, to confirm the a priori assumption of an Oedipally determined link between a man's childhood at the hands of his father and his adult behaviors, successes, and failures. (The compliantly unobtrusive wife and mother is a convenience, although her presence or absence, involvement or abnegation of responsibility would, read through Oedipal lenses, in the end add up to the same thing.) The artifactual weight of straps and halters, texts and drawings somehow legitimates the evidence by which psychic damage may be asserted and assessed, as if such exhibits give forensic testimony, more tangible metonymies for spiritual and sexual injury than the merely linguistic. And more obliquely we have what the historian dreams of finding: a *humanly located* cause and effect system that is more than merely deterministic – the historian's complaint against pure psychoanalytic readings of character – because it shows the effects of the particular historical circumstan-

---

[4] Israels, *Schreber: Father and Son*, xiii.

ces in the case. 'Individuality . . . is just that out of which history is made,' says Collingwood, 'The historian need not and cannot (without ceasing to be an historian) emulate the scientist in searching for the cause or laws of events . . . This does not mean that words like 'cause' are necessarily out of place in reference to history; it only means that they are there in a special sense . . . The cause of the event, for him, means the thought of the mind of the person by whose agency the event came about: and this is not something other than the event, it is the inside of the event itself.'[5] The tethers between father and son seem so iron-clad as to be legitimately supervalent; the interpretation of specifics may be disputed after the fact of the Oedipal connection having been doubly verified (by Freud, by Niederland, et al.) as a systemic truth which asserts itself as irrefutable.

And more than that, we have Freud's license to take the central text, the memoirs, as sufficient, equal to the man himself; and we have Freud's mandate as well to make the next turn of the screw, so that the text equals the man equals Oedipus. Freud asserts that the nature of Schreber's illness itself licenses the study of Schreber's text as both sufficient and 'true': because paranoia does not yield to analysis, the fixed terms of a written text may be read as revelatory. As Freud says:

The psychoanalytic investigation of paranoia would be altogether impossible if the patients themselves did not possess the peculiarity of betraying (in a distorted form, it is true) precisely those things which other neurotics keep hidden as a secret. Since paranoiacs cannot be compelled to overcome their internal resistances, and since in any case they only say what they choose to say, it follows that this is precisely a disorder in which a written report or a printed case history can take the place of personal acquaintance with the patient. For this reason, I think it is legitimate to base analytic interpretations upon the case history of a patient suffering from paranoia (or more precisely, from dementia paranoides) whom I have never seen, but who has written his own case history and brought it before the public in print.[6]

The significance of Freud's gesture cannot be overstated. He has in one authoritative move pronounced the text and the man equivalent and has acted accordingly, despite his experience as a

---

[5] R. G. Collingwood, *The Idea of History*, ed. Jan Van Der Dussen (Oxford: Clarendon Press, 1993), 150, 214–15.
[6] Sigmund Freud, *Three Case Histories* (New York: Collier, 1963), 83–84.

clinician; the text and the man are personifications of each other. Even resistance to his reading occurs from inside it: Lothane says, 'The more I read and the more I compared Freud's great interpretation with what Schreber said, the more it struck me that Freud was not listening to Schreber, not, as he would say later, interpreting *from* Schreber but interpreting *into* Schreber, projecting his ideas into him.'[7] Freud's 'great interpretation' gives the *Memoirs* such unequivocal status that it opens the field to an ongoing system of prosopopeia, whereby father as well as son are taken as fully embodied in their various texts (all those figures – of men, of machinery – that fill the father's text will serve to make this metonymic contiguity all the more compelling); Freud recognizes that he must read through the anamorphosis of the paranoiac's skewed telling of his truth, but holding the key to the code, he is prepared to translate.

This equivalency between the body and the body of the text is a standard motif in literature, but it is seldom so specifically and authoritatively licensed as this. It could be said that Freud's gesture recapitulates a move standard within the psychoanalytic language game: it happens elsewhere that a partial object – the phallus, for example – is conceptualized first as a part, and then as a part for the whole, and then as a whole object with full, motivating significance unto itself; this is metonymizing with a twist, as the contiguous but partial thing first felt as representative becomes no longer merely representative but initiatory in significance. In this infusion of the meaning of the whole into the partial object, psychoanalysis and schizophrenia may be said to share an investment in what Freud calls 'organ speech,' for if in schizophrenia the patient's relation to a bodily organ 'has abrogated to itself the representation of the whole content' of her thoughts, in psychoanalysis the phallus either does the talking or shows up missing to prove language insufficient.[8] Freud did not invent this sleight of hand, which is typical to theoretizing and dependent upon the convenient amnesias upon which systems are built (it may, indeed, be fundamental to the way language works), but he is unique in his authority to so connect word and body.

[7] Lothane, *In Defense of Schreber*, 5.
[8] Sigmund Freud, 'The Unconscious,' in *The Standard Edition of the Complete Psychological Works of Sigmund Freud*, vol. XIV, trans. James Strachey (London: Hogarth Press, 1957), 198.

This assimilation of historical figure to written language is historiography's lost dream of authority, as it makes the document a fully adequate artifact, a potent metonymy which carries out in condensed but not cryptographic form the main component of a given history; it accomplishes two Herculean tasks at once, in that it superimposes history and humanness and in that it superimposes language and truth. It is as if in so conflating (human) figure and story, the problematic gap between tropological fancy and testimonial transparency is closed without ever having to look over into the abyss. The equation is positively elegant, and if it can work to decode Schreber's floridly inventive poetic language into case history and syntagmatic order it can work anywhere, on any text: man, text, story are one, with certain markers – 'paranoid,' 'homosexual' – falling into place around that Oedipal jar in Tennessee, and thus all figural complexities smooth themselves into the surface of this aerially defined topography. Freud's failure to be seduced into a consideration of the specifics of Schreber's language has been greeted with indignation: 'It should be noted that Judge Schreber's destiny was not merely that of being sodomized, while still alive, by the rays from heaven,' say Deleuze and Guattari, 'but also that of being posthumously oedipalized by Freud. From the enormous political, social, and historical content of Schreber's delirium, *not one word is retained*, as though the libido did not bother itself with such things.'[9] But in fact, this eliding of text to man depends upon, necessitates, and authorizes all at once Freud's suave reductionism to clinical typology (a hermeneutic circle, indeed); the archeological density of the language, both from a tropological and symbolic point of view and from the point of view of 'political, social, and historical content,' resists the necessary linearities of clinical, historical and juridical narrative.

Schreber himself might be given here an opportunity to speak to this system of rhetorical necessity, for he seems to apprehend the relationship between language and power that Freud's appropriation of the *Memoirs* reveals so candidly, and his description of the 'basic language' could be used as a primer by which one learns about language and its vicissitudes in both the historical and the analytic discourse. (Its companion piece might be Freud's own

[9] Gilles Deleuze and Felix Guattari, *Anti-Oedipus: Capitalism and Schizophrenia*, trans. Robert Hurley, Mark Seem, and Helen R. Lane (Minneapolis: University of Minnesota Press, 1989), 57.

text, 'The Antithetical Meaning of Primal Words': 'In Latin *altus* means "high" and "deep" . . . Our "bos" ("bad") is matched by a word "bass" ("good"); in Old Saxon "bat" ("good") corresponds to the English "bad" . . . We can compare the German words "stumm" ["dumb"] and "Stimme" ["voice"], and so on.')[10] Schreber writes, 'The souls to be purified learnt during purification the language spoken by God Himself, the so-called 'basic language', a somewhat antiquated but nevertheless powerful German, characterized particularly by a wealth of euphemisms (for instance, reward in the reverse sense for punishment, poison for food, juice for venom, unholy for holy, etc.)' (49–50). Schreber's sense of what he calls 'euphemisms' is not only a description of how 'poetic' language (and in fact *all* language) tends to work – through paradox and ambiguity, with tropes like syllepses and oxymorons that function by establishing a truth through apparent contradiction, through a system of metaphors in which the double term provokes an unnamed third presence that is neither one nor the other, through lapses into catachresis, structures of metaphor whose disjunctions produce images of greater or lesser monstrosity. It is as well a description of how a 'God's' language can be whatever it wants to be, including obtuse or forgetful, because it emanates from absolute power (as Freud points out, *'sacer'* means both 'sacred' and 'accursed,' a double meaning performed throughout Schreber's discussions of his God);[11] and in concordance with this sense it is a recognition that language, as Freud himself deeply understood, can facilitate this doubleness at a most basic and pervasive level.

In one sense Schreber's understanding is diurnal, the effect of experience, i.e. it is historically based; he is physically located in an environment that actualizes these double meanings within the doctor/patient relationship where, for example, 'juice' or 'food' – that which is ingested – might in a very ordinary way be felt by the recipient as 'poison' or 'venom': sodium bromide (64), chloral hydrate (65), potassium bromide, etc. are given as therapeutic but felt in very significant ways as an assault on the body.[12] And in the very notion of 'asylum' is embodied the double meaning of

[10] *The Standard Edition of the Complete Psychological Works of Sigmund Freud*, vol. XI, trans. James Strachey (London: Hogarth Press, 1957), 155–61.
[11] Freud, 'The Antithetical Meaning of Primal Words,' 159.
[12] See Lothane, *In Defense of Schreber*, 34–35.

reward and punishment, protection and incarceration. Schreber, as usual, knows and tells both sides of the story that his evaluators inevitably reduce to a unilateral reading. He has been a judge, a *Senatspräsident*, he is as he writes a writer, and as he speaks an effective advocate of his own release, and he is by virtue of his tutelage a madman, without authority: and he does not in this text dichotomize the two forms of knowledge ('male' and 'female'), either structurally or imagistically because he feels his vision holistically as 'truth.' And here, Schreber does what the analysts and the psychobiographers cannot do, because they are Oedipally bound to structures of either/or.

Schreber himself reveals the immense power his language holds to thwart convention and alter his physical reality if he can only make it be heard. Certainly the success of his suit for recission of tutelage has a great deal to do with his making the judiciary *listen* to him long enough to become confused by his potently ratiocinative madness; in a 1902 'Postscript' to the *Memoirs*, after his successful suit for freedom and just before his discharge, Schreber writes, 'Miracles and the talking voices continue as before. The slowing down of the voices has progressed further so that the words are hardly understandable . . . but the voices are still *continuous* . . . The miracles continue to take on a more and more harmless character . . . The sensation of temporary thinning and furrowing of the bony substance of my skull persists, and can hardly be only subjective . . . By continual counting I can also prevent bellowing almost completely in public places,' and so on (247). The court doesn't think him 'sane' any more than his attending physician Guido Weber does, but under the force of his language and his presence, textually and physically, neither can they reduce him to a standard category.[13] He enforces oxymoron, proving himself to be a competent madman and a hallucinatory realist, and by walking out the door of the asylum a free man he takes this linguistic and epistemological virus out into the world of work and law. That Freud himself felt the specific pleasures of Schreber's text is revealed in his use of Schreberisms in letters to friends, thus translating terms of the basic language into a meta-text of self-irony and satiric implication; his relatively ascetic

---

[13] See *Memoirs*, 267–83, 315–27, for Weber's three reports, of 9 December 1899, 28 November 1900, and 5 April 1902; for the 'Judgment of the Royal Superior Country Court Dresden' of 14 July 1902, see 329–56.

case study is not, then, based on insensitivity to the linguistic impact of Schreber's work, nor, as one will know from reading Freud's own texts, is it based on any rhetorical, imaginative, or poetic insufficiency on Freud's part; it is instead, as are to some extent all texts, the willful wresting of terms to fit the needs of the situation.[14]

In fact, Freud and the psychobiographers cannot *afford* to listen to the *Memoirs'* siren song, which is so performative that it threatens to subvert rational response: as Schreber says, as if to parody psychoanalysis's own appropriation of common-language terms for its new discourse, the souls speak of 'soul murder' for two reasons – 'for lack of a better term, using a term already in current usage, and because of their innate tendency to express themselves hyperbolically,' and their canny double understanding of pedagogy (the language of history – current usage) and of poetry (hyperbole) is powerfully subversive of unilateral order (35). If one actually listens to Schreber's text without the psychotherapeutic translator-machine in place, one does not merely see, but feels the way that, as J. L. Austin would say, language puts two shining skids beneath our metaphysical feet: 'To feel the firm ground of prejudice slipping away is exhilarating, but brings its revenges.'[15] Heard for itself, Schreber's *Memoirs* is history's and historiography's nightmare, as it proves humor and even irony inseparable from a virtually messianic sincerity (any careful reader knows that irony is often the most palpable sincerity, and the more unstable the more revelatory), as it proves personas, and even gendering itself, to be both self-consciously crafted and the products of metamorphic necessity, as it proves tropological language – the interdependent transformations of metaphor and metonymy – to be integrated within and necessary to truth-telling, as it proves logic to be as serviceable to madmen as to civil servants, who are in this case the same man. But, once reduced to type, Schreber's living text can then bring earlier and correlative documents into the discourse as live respondents – the father's most particularly, but the whole textual system is animated by the myth, if not the specifics, of Schreber's magic word.

The obvious metatextual questions that Freud's assessment

[14] See Peter Gay, *Freud: A Life for Our Times* (New York: Doubleday, 1988), 279.
[15] J. L. Austin, *Philosophical Papers* (Oxford: Clarendon Press, 1990), 241; *How to Do Things With Words* (Cambridge: Harvard University Press, 1975), 61.

raises may thus be bracketed in favor of a consideration of its authoritative effect (Freud has taken, without reserve, Schreber's word on the matter of his own illness and has done so with no attempt at clinical verification. He has responded to Schreber's text as if it is absolutely veracious, as if it is the necessary and inevitable translation into words of the truth of Schreber's physical and psychic condition. This, in the case of madness and in the case of literary texts, is a procedure not without its dangers); and the effect is that, with such formidible authority as Freud's as back-up, biographers and analysts may slice the Gordian knot and say with Israels, 'the sincerity and preciseness with which Paul Schreber wrote down his psychotic experiences are beyond all doubt' (xiv). The one man, Daniel Paul, becomes inextricable from his typography and he is as well the end of a Oedipal line of Daniel Schrebers extending backwards into the historical past. Ironically, it is as if Freud has translated Schreber's metonymic intuitions into his own assertion of textual sufficiency, for Schreber himself provides the license by which the whole of memory is condensed within each element of a series of separate articulations: 'Circumstances seem to be such,' says Schreber, 'that *every single nerve of intellect represents the total mental individuality of a human being*, that the sum total of recollections is as it were inscribed on each single nerve of intellect' (45). (And for the psychobiographer who would confirm paternal influence Schreber gives authority as well, in his footnote: 'The male seed contains a paternal nerve and combines with a nerve taken from the mother's body to form a newly created entity. This new entity – the child to be – thus recreates anew the father and the mother, perhaps more the former than the latter, in turn receives new impressions in its lifetime and then transmits this newly acquired individuality to its descendants' (45).)

Freud himself licenses an analysis that, from his 1911 beginning to its post-1959 ends, will take place almost entirely within the realm of textual assessment: we have here a series of stories being told about a written and finalized story, for Schreber himself disappears into obscurity, the records of post-Sonnenstein years scanty, the details of his last illness, his final institutionalization, and his death non-existent. Biographers like Israels and Lothane were able to speak to Schreber's sister, Anna Jung, who died at age 104, and to use the texts, produced by earlier inquiries, based on interviews with people who had known the Schreber family, but

'Schreber' becomes history even before his death, a proper name on a title page. And this conflation of name, page, and man validates retroactively the privileging of the paternal texts that came before ('It is possible that Dr. Schreber may still be living to-day,' says Freud, but it finally does not much matter for his purposes (84)). And Schreber's book is the perfect book for this game, a Prospero's book of infinite possibility because its truth is not in what it specifically and overtly asserts to be true. It is at once considered completely authoritative in its articulation of the terms of its madness and, because it is itself mad, it may at the same time exist as the institutionalized madman exists, which is to say *without* authority, without the power to threaten, without the power to convince at the level it wishes to convince (Schreber's delusions are real for him, but he cannot persuade his keepers of this truth).

It is thus a completely seductive, completely violable book chock full of rich details that may be deployed (or not) in any old way the current authorities need to deploy them. The *Memoirs* may or may not be a victim's story in the sense of its attempting to document a real 'reality' whose very nature precludes outside verification: 'It is the nature of a victim not to be able to prove that one has been done a wrong,' says Lyotard. 'A plaintiff is someone who has incurred damages and who disposes of the means to prove it. One becomes a victim if one loses these means.'[16] And Schreber's case is even more complex than this, since his affective power and the very terms of the critical argument reside in perceiving him, not as the victim he claims himself to be, of Flechsig, of God, but as 'victim' – as the victim of his own terrible madness, or as the victim of his own terrible madness as the result of having been victimized by his father. One may, in this case, not believe Schreber and feel oneself as humane in any event. Not having access to the same objects of cognition as Schreber, one can only choose from models of discourse which use words that are more or less hostile to the notion of the text as true (the shaman might say 'vision,' and the psychoanalyst might say 'hallucination, experientially induced,' and the psychiatrist might say 'delusion, potentially genetic in origin,' and the man in the street might say 'he's crazy,' and these terms will each adjudicate the

---

[16] Jean-François Lyotard, *The Differend: Phrases in Dispute,* trans. Georges Van Den Abbeele (Minneapolis: University of Minnesota Press, 1988), 8.

case regarding Schreber's madness using different criteria which also impose upon it, among other things, a variable moral status). Schreber claims that Flechsig and God's Rays are attempting to murder his soul; Freud claims that Schreber is paranoid. We – the materialist, evidentially inclined people – generally decide for Freud and against Schreber, whose 'truth' is the truth of his madness speaking through him and not the truth of what he says. The only way that Schreber's self-perceived truths may be arbitrated is within a system that will not allow the terms by which he himself validates the reality of his experience, and those, like Niederland and Schatzman, who work to ameliorate his position do not (cannot) do so through vindication but only through the establishing of extenuating claims.

Without exiting from the seriousness of this analysis, one could, in fact, say that Schreber and his texts are a bit like a woman traditionally perceived and articulated, a connection Schreber himself communicates quite explicitly: the effect of the *Memoirs* is performatively powerful but discredited in advance at the level of sane, dependable rationality. Schreber's condition is clearly that of a victim, but as is usual with women the question must be, 'the victim of *what*?' Is he victimized by a weakness emanating from within; does he therefore ask – because he wishes to be violated, lays himself open to the voluptuousness of his nature – to be victimized? Schreber feels himself becoming female, becoming an elaborated, decorative text whose constative power paradoxically diminishes as the strength of his conviction of truth increases. In the tradition that sees rhetorical decoration as female and as whorish, Schreber's (body) language is spoken through women's clothes and cheap jewelry; his text is similarly elaborated, although the authorities strip it down for business. And once again, Schreber proves prophetic, for when he asserts that 'God Himself' would either instigate or abet a soul murder in which Schreber's body would be handed over 'in the manner of a female harlot' he could be read at one significant level as predicting the fate of his own text (77).

For one suspects that Father Freud and his followers can allow Schreber's book very little leeway, for fear that the hearing of it on its own terms would mean madness, or desire, or some shared intuition of femaleness: one would have to believe the victim and we know from hard experience what this means for Freud in the way of (his own) existential, historical, and psychoanalytic complexity. 'Paranoia' is in this case a potentially double-edged term, for, on the one hand, it is what the victim who cannot prove his case is adjudged to suffer: as Lyotard says, 'If there is nobody to adduce the proof, nobody to admit it, and/or if the argument which upholds it is judged to be absurd, then the plaintiff is dismissed . . . He or she becomes a victim. If he or she persists in invoking this wrong as if it existed, the others . . . will easily be able to make her pass for mad. Doesn't paranoia confuse the *As if it were the case* with the *It is the case*?'[17] On the other hand, it may be the result of the oedipalized anxieties of the evaluators who themselves lose the finesse both to distinguish between Schreber's postulations (poetic, symbolic, metaphoric) 'As if it were the case' and his constative assertions, 'it is the case' and to recognize the interplay between the two formulations.

Hermaphroditic, Schreber communicates himself as outside the normative terms of the Oedipal conflict, but the analytic responses to his feminization tend to reinstate the dialectic by which (psycho)historiography proceeds: God/Father/Presence/Doctor beneath whose monolithic and weighty authority antitheses proliferate like worms. Beneath the penetrative rays that come to him from masculine powers named Flechsig, God, Ormuzd, Ariman, etc., Schreber feels himself changing, in an eternal process of becoming female. When he calls himself a 'Hyperborean woman' it is perhaps a way of communicating the multiple and contradictory, thoroughly enriched levels at which this transformation should be perceived (93): as a metamorphosis within time because it is endless – Hyperborean space can never be reached – and outside of time because a Hyperborean woman is eternal; as a golden place in a golden age, behind the north wind, erotically pleasurable, and as the north wind itself, arctic, frigid; as, in other words, a simultaneity of conditions whose terms refute the paternal model. Yet the analysts, returning the metamorphosis to standard terms, cannot see that in another sense Schreber has hallucinated historiography's dream of a single body that is both within time (history) and outside of time (eternality); under standard terms, this eternally becoming female is a form of erasure (history, disappearing before one's eyes), the worst of all horrors.

[17] *Ibid.*, 8.

At best they join Lothane in pointing out that the Tiresias fantasy is 'a universal fantasy of mankind, sane or insane,' since Tiresias' answer to the question of whose pleasure was greater during intercourse was 'women's' (a response, of course, for which s/he got struck blind).[18]

Schreber himself articulates this 'unmanning' as complex in its implications; it is not so simple a thing for Schreber as 'emasculation' and not so simple as 'homosexuality' and not so simple as simple degradation. The readings that flatten and reduce Schreber's fantasy of unmanning by construing it unambiguously as emasculation do so at the expense of Schreber's own views of the subject, and, indeed, of other, similar accounts by non-institutionalized, apparently functional men. Ed Cohen, in 'The Double Lives of Man: Nineteenth-Century Representation of Ec-centric Masculinities,' reads what might be called proto-coming out stories by John Addington Symonds and an anonymous Hungarian physician who contributed his own case history for the second edition of Krafft-Ebing's *Psychopathia Sexualis*. The physician writes, 'I felt that . . . the genitals had shrunken, the pelvis broadened, the breasts swollen out, a feeling of unspeakable delight came over me.' Symonds invents the term 'dipsychia' to describe the doubleness he feels that he has cultivated in disguising his 'inner and real character' with an overlay of 'commonplace cheerfulness.'[19] These accounts illustrate the willfulness necessary to keeping the semantic faith in terms like 'homosexual' or 'paranoid' or 'manhood.' For Schreber, becoming a woman is necessarily embarrassing, although after his release he maintains the right to dress as a woman when he wishes. His gender trouble is both painful to contemplate, given his cultural circumstances, and pleasurable to feel – like the doctor's 'unspeakable delight,' it comes as a 'soul-voluptousness' that soothes his tortured thoughts. And it is not only nullification that *he* feels but multiplication: he is moving toward the capacity for a pregnancy that will save the world. *Schreber* can see the compensations in the matter, *I* can see the compensations in the matter, as Masson and Schatzman point out, a shaman or mystic would see the compensations in the matter, but one who subscribes to the dominant narrative of

---

[18] Lothane, *In Defense of Schreber*, 335–36.
[19] Ed Cohen, 'The Double Lives of Men,' *Victorian Studies*, 36, 3 (Spring 1993), 353–76.

power/powerlessness, form/shapelessness, universal/particular will inevitably see unmanning as emasculation. Habits of language and an entire system of metaphor have stacked the deck; add to this the specifics of the Oedipal tale, including castration, and the terms are set.

Schreber is felt by the biographers, and the historians, and the analysts as a cautionary figure, and their discomfort with his fluid gendering lets one know that they take his warning to heart. 'Schreber' taken as a poetics is one thing, but taken historiographically he is another. The historian, male or female, who wishes to keep masculinity – i.e. authority – intact simply cannot afford to give up his asymptotic progress towards (becoming) the Father, for what would history-telling become if there were not this unchanging presence with its threat of castration to keep order among the welter of detail and change? (As Gay points out, the whole painful Oedipal experience is that which must occur to bring the son to manhood: 'it generates the incest taboo and the pangs of conscience in the child and thus passes on to the sons the wisdom of the fathers'.[20]) 'Clio' is, after all, feared at the two predictable levels of disruption for which women are famed: as frigid and as overly desirous. In the second, implicit, fantasy she is susceptible – heir to all the frailties of her sex, violable and, worse, potentially just whorish enough to *want* some untoward excitement – and thus she must be guarded by the paternal guardians. The psychohistorians, says Barzun, 'attempt to rescue Clio from pitiable maidenhood by artificial insemination,' a method 'they know is nothing new.' In Peter Gay's version of this dubious metaphor, 'Clio on the couch does not respond . . . She just lies there. We find the disheartening implications of her obstinate, frustrating passivity spread across the pages of psychohistorical writings' (if she moved there would, of course, be equal trouble in the other direction).[21] For Bloch, anxious historians 'wish only to spare Clio's chastity from the profanation of present controversy,' although 'This is to rate our self-control rather low.'[22] And Barzun concludes *Clio and the Doctors* (an unsettling title under the circumstances), by protesting (too much, one thinks), 'Clio is not a

[20] Peter Gay, *Freud for Historians*, (Oxford University Press, 1985), 98.
[21] Peter Gay, *Freud for Historians*, (Oxford University Press, 1985), 182.
[22] Marc Bloch, *The Historian's Craft*, trans. Peter Putnam (New York: Vintage Books, 1953), 37.

good mixer or of easy virtue' and so while some may fear that 'history may also be tumbled netherwards,' in the end 'Clio will again be found among [the muses], *virgo intacta*' (this later metaphor, preceded by Barzun's image of history under the curative scalpel, is positively unsettling).[23] Tumbling netherwards, right to the erotic jackpot: if historians claim to disapprove of what they take to be Freud's thoroughly sexualized version of human nature, clearly it is not from lack of imagination regarding the subject. The displacement onto psychohistory of the burden of this erotic charge is very convenient, but one cannot help but feel that the source of anxiety in the matter comes from within the larger disciplinary matrix of historiography proper.

To free assumptions about the unconscious from the representational order given it by the Oedipal story would be to exit temporality and therefore to exit history, and if a certain terrorism (impending castration) is necessary to enforce this order, so be it: 'We must speak of 'castration' in the same way we speak of oedipalization, whose crowning moment it is,' says Deleuze, 'castration designates the operation by which psychoanalysis castrates the unconscious, injects castration into the unconscious. Castration as a practical operation on the unconscious is achieved when the thousand breaks-flows of desiring-machines – all positive, all productive – are projected into the same mythical space, the unary stroke of the signifier.'[24] (This is an observation given weight by Gay's hopeful conclusion to a discussion of the Oedipal phase: 'I have drawn this developmental sketch to underscore my conviction that a sociology of the unconscious is now a realistic possibility.'[25]) In this schema, 'becoming a woman' is emasculation, as it is felt to cut away the most comforting and necessary prop of all. The Tiresian view must be rejected, then, for the forgetfulness of a fully masculinized approach, perhaps precisely *because* of his fantacized answer to that $64,000 question of who has more fun in bed.

Schreber also epitomizes the rise and fall Peter Loewenberg has announced as the psychohistorian's first clue and his final evidence in the matter of an Oedipal crack-up; more generally, Schreber caricatures and thus substantiates in bold strokes his-

[23] Jacques Barzun, *Clio and the Doctors* (University of Chicago Press, 1974), 14, 155, 158.   [24] Deleuze and Guattari, *Anti-Oedipus*, 60–61.
[25] Gay, *Freud for Historians*, 162.

toriography's structural predisposition toward the Oedipal trajectory from relative obscurity to power and back to defeat, and his clinically assessed paranoia is merely the limit case in a system of analysis that has typically read paranoia into the power-seeking equation so as to shape and justify the necessary narrative of success and failure.[26] We have in Daniel Paul Schreber a figure whose political, professional, and social eminence, demonstrated in his precocious attainment of the appointment of *Senatspräsident*, seems to have been thwarted at its height by the very qualities that had brought him to success: 'I started to sleep badly,' says Schreber, 'at the very moment when I was able to feel that I had largely mastered the difficulties of settling down in my new office and in my new residence, etc.' (64). In other words, Schreber fits Loewenberg's candid faith in the telos represented in the section, 'Those Wrecked by Success,' in Freud's essay 'Some Character Types Met With in Psychoanalytic Work': 'In 1916,' says Loewenberg, 'Freud wrote a short paper crucial for the understanding of ego psychology and highly relevant to historians; it is his section "Those Wrecked by Success" in "Some Character-Types Met With in Psychoanalytic Work."' 'In both historical studies and psychoanalysis there is no more productive or crucial question than "Why now?"'[27] And indeed, Freud's essay, with its fluid movements among historicizing, literary analysis, and psychoanalysis, is paradigmatic for the psychohistorian and the psychobiographer, if not more generally for the historian: it achieves at every level from direct assertion to subtextual effect that collapsing of clinical, material, or documentary evidence into (literary) narrative upon which the historian depends. Freud here explicitly authorizes a full and unambiguous reciprocity between clinical and literary characterization, and he implicitly justifies this move by asserting a deterministic primacy of the Oedipus Complex that spills as inevitably into literature as into life.

Loewenberg's specific advocacy of this section in Freud's essay on psychoanalytic types opens a trunk packed tight with the stuff historiography depends upon: its master narrative, its method, its

---

[26] See, for example, Harold Laswell, 'The Selective Effect of Personality on Political Participation,' in *Studies In the Scope and Method of 'The Authoritarian Personality,'* eds. Richard Christie and Marie Jahoda (Glencoe: Free Press, 1954).

[27] Peter Loewenberg, *Decoding the Past: The Psychohistorical Approach* (New York: Knopf, 1983), 31.

engagement with temporality in the face of an overabundance of material possibility, its relationship to evidence. 'Those Wrecked by Success' enacts in condensed form the evidential faith in written language and characterization on which psychohistory must be based; its rhetorical strategies mimic the dramatic unfolding crucial to the telling of any good story, history and case-history included; its analytic interventions in complex narrative systems license the historian's necessary fiction of a defining moment around which the story may form. (Again: 'In both historical studies and psychoanalysis there is no more productive or crucial question than "Why now?"') Freud conducts his analysis of those wrecked by success by a smooth elision of case history into history into the fictions embodied in *Macbeth* and Ibsen's *Rosmerholm* (and his choice of drama, removed as it is from embedding within narrative, and his choice of these particular dramas, historically and realistically fraught as they are, is significant in more than one way; it reifies what Deleuze and Guattari have seen as the organizational effect of oedipalizing: 'The unconscious ceases to be what it is – a factory, a workshop – to become a theater, a scene and its staging. And not even an *avant-garde* theater . . . but a classical theater, the classical order of representation.'[28]). His analysis of *Macbeth* begins with a question – does Lady Macbeth fail because she is worn out or from some 'deeper motivation' – which he immediately follows with the disingenuous assertion, 'It seems to me impossible to come to any decision.' He goes on to cite the historical circumstances of the play as a *pièce d'occasion*, and to reveal *Macbeth*'s 'remarkable analogies to the actual situation' reflected in Elizabeth's childlessness, and her execution of Mary Stuart. Thus establishing a link between historical and fictional circumstance, Freud conflates this narrative with the fictional characters' personal histories by moving seamlessly among them all. And, in fact, he does come to a decision regarding the deeper motivation for failure, and he concludes the section thus:

After this long digression into literature, let us return to clinical experience – but only to establish in a few words the complete agreement between them. Psychoanalytic work teaches that the forces of conscience which induce illness in consequence of success, instead of, as normally, in

[28] Deleuze and Guattari, *Anti-Oedipus*, p. 55.

consequence of frustration, are closely connected with the Oedipus Complex, the relation to father and mother – as perhaps, indeed, is all our sense of guilt in general.[29]

Two birds with one stone: the text, whether literary or documentary, will reveal the truth, and the truth shall be revealed as Oedipal.

Oedipal psychobiography

One thus sees in the Schreber case how the chiaroscuro of psychobiography comes about, as evidence either locates itself within the prevailing paradigm (the father's texts, the son's *Memoirs*, the court documents, Freud's contemporaneous study, all now read through the lens of a direct causal relationship between father and son) or ceases to exist. The father/son story may be qualified, supplemented, and embellished, and thus the generation of competing Schreber studies. But attempts at radical correction or usurpation of this dominant Oedipal narrative must contend, and never with complete success, with the seductive antitheses deployed to construct a balanced, well-buttressed, and dramatic story; both Israels and Lothane, the two most recent participants in the biographical warfare, take serious issue with what they feel to be the overly simple Niederland/Schatzman correlation between parental sadism and filial illness, but, bound within the terms of this discourse, they recapitulate it and, in their own procedural squabbling, reify it as well. In fact, the generation of multiple readings of the same story in this case is more than ordinarily well-matched to the sadisms and overmanning it evaluates or dismisses. Collingwood's discussion of the historian's autonomy as it it manifested most strikingly in historical criticism (corrective historiography meant to undo past historiographic mistakes and inadequacies) lays the terms out quite clearly under which the Schreber discourse has been conducted: 'As natural science finds its proper method when the scientist . . . puts Nature to the question, tortures her . . . in order to wring from her answers to his own questions, so history finds its proper method when the historian puts his authorities in the witness-box, and by cross-

[29] Sigmund Freud, 'Some Character Types Met With in Psychoanalytic Work,' in *The Standard Edition of the Complete Psychological Works of Sigmund Freud*, vol. XIV, trans. James Strachey (London: Hogarth Press, 1957), 331.

examining extorts from them information which in their original statements they have withheld, either because they did not wish to give it or because they did not possess it.'[30] The act of re-evaluation itself is provocative of conflict, and within the Schreber case the polarized father/son relationship erects a sturdy set of binary oppositions leading one to the satisfaction of narrative closure; its Sophoclean urgency obscures the fact that this closure will always be at the expense of any 'extraneous' detail that might vitiate or contradict this most compelling of stories. The dichotomies of love/hate, power/powerlessness, male/female, feminine/masculine, sadism/masochism, father/son, God/supplicant/doctor/patient, the persecutor/persecuted provide an embracing system in which exploration of detail may be carried out snugly, in teleological safety.

Dark and light, black and white, father and son, timelessness and temporality, universal and specific: the dual texts of father and son invite antiphonal reading, and their themes are so complementary that they often enact structual and narrative schisms in the texts in which they appear. Morton Schatzman, for example, proves in *Soul Murder* his ability to tell a good story (the book sold very well) as he focuses first on the father alone; when, however, he opens the field both to the father's and the son's texts simultaneously, the narrative structure itself breaks apart into the stark juxtaposition of relevant fragments from each source.[31] As if under the spell of some ontotheological necessity, Schatzman yields his narrative voice to the father, and the relative seamlessness of his story is replaced with antiphonal voices in which the son sings soprano to his father's bass. For a moment the subject/object bifurcation intrinsic to the historiographical process is laid bare in Schatzman's text with virtually allegorical precision: the Father, universal and omnipotent, synchronous as a force, and the Son, particularized, feminized, feeling himself as literally metamorphic, the embodiment of change, Father and Son Schreber hypostasizing a marriage of metaphysics and history. In the analytic literature what was at the very least only tacit in Schreber's *Memoirs* is announced as fact: 'Fleschig' and 'God' are names for the Father in Schreber's text (and as Freud is the first to point out, God and Father are so reciprocal as to become one: 'Such

---

[30] Collingwood, *The Idea of History*, 237.   [31] Schatzman, *Soul Murder*, 41–52.

a father as this was by no means unsuitable for transfiguration into a God in the affectionate memory of his son' (127)). This is an elegant reductionism that capitulates without apparent skepticism to stereotypical symbolic values; on a skeptical view it seems, in fact, the inevitable, knee-jerk memorializing of the Father, an act of filial piety as inevitable as the 'Bless you' that is muttered after every sneeze. Certainly, one could at least say that the inevitable conflation of Father and God within an unbroken chain of being suggests the ontotheological bias in historiography's standard discourse of great men. Such chronic memorializing conjures Presence into being with each reiteration of the Oedipal tale,

But as Lyotard points out in *Heidegger and 'the jews'*, the memorial is in its selectivity most paradoxically and necessarily forgetful of all that might threaten its iconographic status. Lyotard examines what he calls the 'politics of forgetting':

But as far as forgetting is concerned, this memory of the memorial is intensely selective; it requires the forgetting of that which may question the community and its legitimacy. This is not to say that memory does not address this problem, quite the contrary. It represents, may and must represent, tyranny, discord, civil war, the mutual sharing of shame, and conflicts born of rage and hate.[32]

And yet, he says, even so, the memorial as representation must be a sublation, 'an elevation . . . that enthralls and removes . . . We might say in today's idiom: an elevation that wraps up (emballe) in both senses of the word.'

Selective amnesia is permissible, indeed essential, within a metaphysical structure, for the particularities under consideration are already, before the fact, paradigmatically determined by the apprehension of a fixed term which cannot be altered by empirical means: this is a structure that madness makes manifest through virtual caricature – indeed, it is the means by which madness is diagnosed – for madness, as Schreber's case illustrates, often erects a precise and rigorous logic on the foundation of a (mistaken, insufficient, non-contextualized) organizing truth.[33] There are gaps in the madman's memory of the world so that he can stick to his story. Aporia is harmless enough when the path is well marked and the goal in view, for one's momentum will carry

[32] Jean François Lyotard, *Heidegger and 'The Jews'*, trans. Andreas Michel and Mark S. Roberts (Minneapolis: University of Minnesota Press, 1990), 7–13.
[33] See in this context, Louis A. Sass, *The Paradoxes of Delusion: Wittgenstein, Schreber, and the Schizophrenic Mind* (Ithaca: Cornell University Press, 1994).

him over the holes, and if this is the madman's secret it is also the story-teller's and the historian's comfort. (And Oedipus gets to where he is going precisely by virtue of what he does not know.) Proceeding with the positivist's enthusiasm for gathering material evidence, the modern historian is *not* a pure positivist, and thus he communicates the need to justify his narrative by something other than a set of empirically derived general laws. He must be able not only to ask but to justify the question, 'Why now?'; and implicit in the very question is an assumption that behind action is Fate – the very dilemma of Oedipus himself. Forgetfulness of all the material as yet ungathered or undiscovered is the necessary condition under which cause and effect may flourish, and when Schatzman more or less drops himself from the narrative structure one is left to see the unilateral deployment of cause and effect in all its potency.

One sees this assumption of inevitability as well in Han Israels' biography, *Schreber: Father and Son*, where Israels is so convinced before beginning his task that the link between father and son is directly and explicitly causal that the entire text functions under the claims of a kind of negative capability: Israels will hear the father in ways that the men who have come before him have not been able to hear; he will be a good son, in fact. 'The very case of father and son Schreber,' he says, 'contains an element that goes beyond the naked facts. I refer to the parallels between father Schreber's system of child-rearing and son Schreber's delusions. However, precisely because this is so convincing, *the research that has to be done to determine what may be concluded from it must be all the more painstaking*. Not only do I not offer any new insights: my work is not even on an original subject' (reading statements such as these regarding the Schreber case, one comes to feel powerfully the author's own investment in some personal Oedipal story).[34] This is as unabashed an embracing of a tautology as there could possibly be, with the key to the enigma announced in advance as that which will shape one's apprehension of cause and effect in the matter. Not surprisingly, it echoes precisely the terms of Freud's similar tautology, which says that Schreber's text proves him to be a classic case of paranoia, and thus his text can be read, based on this diagnosis, as a classic case of paranoia. The father/son causality is for Israels so strong a faith that he mimics on a larger

---

[34] Israels, *Schreber: Father and Son*, xx (italics mine).

scale Schatzman's temporary abdication from the shaping of the text into an integrative whole, and he yields structurally to the father; the first section, 'The Schreber Family,' is biographical but it will 'disregard the two most interesting features, that is, Moritz Schreber's ideas on education and Paul Schreber's religious mania' (1); the second section, 'The Reputation of Moritz Schreber,' is recuperative and gives the father the final word, even as the son who utters it ends his book by discrediting his own power in the matter ('I think it is safe to regard the chances of my remarks . . . ever having any influence as negligible' 339). This is not to say that Israels is not contentious regarding the Schreber literature: 'On the existing literature I have almost nothing positive to say: it is my view that the biographical literature is full of errors, I have misgivings about Schatzman's interpretation of the Schreber case, and I shall have even more disparaging things to say about the psychoanalytic literature.'[35] Indeed, he takes on the Schatzman reading of Moritz Schreber and makes a case for the father's rehabilitation from pedagogical terrorist to more human dimensions; tonally, he approximates Collingwood's image of an aggressive lawyer extorting truth from hapless, perjured witnesses. The text itself so powerfully recapitulates at every level an Oedipal dynamic that Israels reifies the very terms of the father/son struggle he has come to set straight.

Israels' Oedipal preoccupations translate into a passive-aggressive text that begins to seem the academic equivalent to Schreber's ambivalence regarding the power that mobilizes him; it is a book fraught with an oxymoronic system of assertive withholding and aggressive negation. It operates, in fact, on the principle of a negative theology in which abnegation of self leads to a revelation, obliquely perceived through the terms of what is not, of an unnameable power.[36] Situating himself as one whose function is receptivity to evidence, Israels makes his task that of undoing past mistakes: 'I hope that with the information I present here I have been able to nip a particular kind of publication in the bud' (xxi). He locates himself throughout the text in negative terms: 'My work is entirely negative in regard to theory . . . I do not offer any new explanation . . . I [do] not offer any new insights' (xx), 'I think it safe to regard the chances of my remarks concerning the history

---

[35] *Ibid.*, xx.   [36] See Deleuze and Guattari, *Anti-Oedipus*, 59–60.

of education ever having any influence as negligible. In the other field of psychiatry, my chances must be if anything still worse, since there I have not been able to suggest even one alternative' (339). He says at one point, 'This section of my introduction does not really belong in this book at all, strictly speaking' (xxi). He takes as his task not so much the revision of past theses regarding the Schreberian players as the nullification of these theses: the section on Pauline Haas Schreber, the mother, provides an excellent example of this tactic (90–95), and section II, on Moritz Schreber, does the same as it discredits what he considers to be the Schatzman school of moralizing calumny while leaving a negative space in which the name of the Father may be felt but not inscribed.

Under the duress of Oedipal anxieties, Israels' reasoning takes on a slightly absurdist tone from beginning to end, so that he says, 'I write about a subject about which much has already been written. If I were to come up up with new biographical information about an unknown nineteenth-century educator and his equally unknown mentally deranged son, that new information would be unimportant' (xx–xxi). Israels' corrective scholarship works to clear the field of over-readings and factual inaccuracies; yet the underlying epistemological stance, which implies his conviction that the 'facts' may be purged of all wrong-headed shaping and distortion and returned to truth, also argues for a certain lack of self-awareness. He speaks with an almost fatalistic voice about the predetermined – indeed, overdetermined – nature of his discourse, and he does so in apparently full faith that the facts he reveals will testify to the Oedipal truth: again, 'The very case of father and son Schreber contains an element that goes beyond the naked facts . . . precisely because this is so convincing, the research that has to be done to determine what may be concluded from it must be all the more painstaking' (xx).

Schreber: Father and Son resigns itself utterly to an Oedipal faith that Israels communicates as both reassuring and totally exasperating (and thus the irascible tone); it enacts, at every level, the Schreberian dilemma of receptivity to a power that is at once murderous and irresistible. Peter Gay argues that an historian's style 'is the pattern in the carpet – the unambiguous indication, to the informed collector, of place and time of origin. It is also the marking on the wings of the butterfly – the infallible signature, to the alert lepidopterist of its species. And it is the involuntary gesture of the witness in the dock – the infallible sign, to the observant lawyer, of concealed evidence.'[37] Whether one uses the wholistic terms – 'style' and 'tone' – of literature or that of psychoanalysis – 'affect' – there are sufficient markers to suggest that Israels writes under significant duress and an equal necessity. If Schatzman fails to see, 'because,' as Israels says, 'his modern aversion to powerful authority blinded him to the insight that an all-powerful despot can be the source not only of misery but also, of joy,' Israels clearly does not fail to see. He apprehends that oedipalized condition of pleasure and pain that Schreber communicates so powerfully in the *Memoirs*, and his own text reproduces that doubleness with uncanny precision as it both exposes and protects the father. And it could be argued that Israels' book is merely a more ingenuous reproduction of Oedipal cause and effect than is generally given in the psychobiographical accounting system.

Those considerations of the Schreber case that would depart from analytic readings of the father/son relationship in order to foreground other factors will find themselves pulled always toward this dominant preoccupation with father and son, toward the irresistible elegance of the Oedipal pair. They are so very iconographically perfect, these two, and if, as Peter Gay asserts, 'The most telling (and most problematic) instance of human nature in action is . . . the Oedipus complex,' they stand as Everyman figures in this drama.[38] So, although it is well within the realm of theoretical possibility that this most compelling of links in the Schreber case obscures other equally valid readings, both psychoanalytic and non-psychoanalytic, the odds are against the creation of other views as long as the broad disciplinary category is '(psycho)history.' As is often the case in psychobiography, lipservice is paid to the crucial concept of overdetermination, even as the procedural moves, the narrative structure, and the rhetorical drive toward enforcing the point erase the memory of overdetermination. Even Gay's sense of overdetermination, which has a sound, commonsensical ring, is difficult to sustain within the overbearing force of oedipalization, which in his own terms transmits 'the wisdom of the fathers'; the Oedipus complex has, says Gay, a 'pedagogic function,' it is a '*school*' which serves 'to tame emotions

---

[37] Gay, *Style in History*, 7.   [38] Gay, *Freud for Historians*, 93.

and channel them in legitimate forms.'[39] By this definition the oedipalized human will exist within a realm of highly complex but more or less standard formulations, and in this context the concept of overdetermination erases all but a handful of possible sets. 'Overdetermination is in fact nothing more than the sensible recognition that a variety of causes – a variety, not infinity – enters into the making of all historical events, and that each ingredient in historical experience can be counted on to have a variety – not infinity – of functions.'[40] The linear structure of historical and biographical narrative, especially as it is deployed under the model of nineteenth-century realism, cannot bear the freight of multiple overdetermination; and psychobiography and psychohistory is distracted as well by the problem of how to superimpose psychoanalytic theory over a narrative that must be kept simple and clean of 'jargon.' In something of a compromised host, then, Oedipal energy may infiltrate and saturate the multiple levels of the text. Fraught with conflicting impulses, the (psycho)historiographer cannot dispose of his ambivalence outside of the system that produces, sustains, and legitimizes it, and thus he yields at every level to the considerable authority of the source he has meant to appropriate to his own ends.

(Psycho)historiography

In effect, Freud's reading of this case through its primary text is the premise from which historiography must begin, for historiography by definition must place significant faith in written documentation, and it cannot afford to yield to the suspicion that documents may tell us more about documents and documentation than about the always partial 'reality' they translate into language; when the man and his word become one, then historiography's chronic problem with memory and forgetfulness – that of humans and that of texts – is solved. In this sense 'Schreber' becomes the ideal historical text, whereby the 'memoir' escapes from its association with the pitfalls of personalized memory and enters the realm of truth. It is *exactly* Schreber's incapacity, his documented and legally sanctioned status as a madman, that eases the evaluator's own paranoia: a competent speaker may

---

[39] *Ibid.*, 98, 95.   [40] *Ibid.*, 187.

author a hoax, or hide within personas, crafted or unconscious, which come at truth aslant; a competent speaker has not only the means to disguise himself but the right, whereas it is the very essence of madness that it is perceived as revelatory because it is read symptomatologically. And Schreber's malaise is paranoia, whose nosology is predicated upon 'the peculiarity of betraying (in a distorted form, it is true) precisely those things which other neurotics keep hidden as a secret': his text provides both the means by which paranoia is discovered and its testimonial. Even the most cryptic manifestations may be translated, because the subject's own authority and, through his legally imposed disenfranchisement his very personhood, are compromised; he no longer *makes* meaning but he *becomes* meaning (and thus 'paranoia' is both the accurate term and its own refutation, as the paranoiac is correct in his intuition that his condition of that of the perpetually victimized).

Schreber, the man-book: he personifies the historiographer's residual fantasy of a living History, hypostasis of the absolute, enacting itself inexorably through the bodies of men in time, proclaiming itself through their texts. Schreber is the truest of prophets, in the sense that he speaks and writes God's language divested of the interventionary meddling of a validated subjectivism. His constative value is unimpeachable at the level of meta-truth; in this higher mathematics the particularities of his textual assertions are both necessary – as the material stuff of which history is made – and discounted before the fact, freeing a more universal history to manifest itself unadorned. Ironically enough, Schreber, who claimed a messianic role and thus proved himself mad, can indeed be felt as salvational as he heals the cranial fizzure between history and metaphysics: the exudant, materially and temporally based specifics of his story, invested within the irrefutable materiality of the *Memoirs* one holds in one's hands, *are also and at the same time* the not-truth that proves metaphysics correct. We could claim from this man a new word, 'schreber,' used to speak of an entire complex in the same way that 'aesthetic' or 'sublime' functions to indicate a system rather than an artifact: the text is one truth, without the capacity for negation and thus completely transparent in its candor, the meta-text is another truth; and the negotiations between the two are felt as negation itself is felt, as an enforcement of reality testing, a choosing of allegiance with the verifiable, the external, the socially and practically acceptable.

Schreber-text is also the obverse figure in history's Oedipal romance with heroes; in pronouncing Schreber's text sufficient, Freud looses truth, historical and otherwise, from its burden of subjective particularity, and he looses heroism from the perennial problem of its necessary blood-kinship with a madness whose status can only be defined retroactively, after the effect of its usurpation of reason has been felt (revisionist history, either immediate or postponed). Schreber's heroism *is* his madness, his madness his heroism; he does what a man has to do, but with a heroism that is the static tincture of itself, having become – by virtue of Schreber's literal confinement, if nothing else – what it is rather than what it does. A heroic victim, he may be read as the quintessence of the Oedipal, as his claiming of himself through the paradoxes of madness may be perceived as at once a most ferocious attack against the father and as an obeisance to the father's enduring authority and power. To read Schreber Oedipally – or, more commonly, to read *about* Schreber in the psychoanalytic and psychobiographical literature – is to perform a devotional, to offer him up as a sacrifice to ontotheological necessity. Fetish or true God, one cannot say, but one thing is certain: every time a man returns to Oedipus as the initiating truth another virile Miltonic angel gets his wings, for to tell the story, to read the world Oedipally, is to *perform* the double act of homage and sacrilege about which the myth speaks.

Schreber's condition of helpless heroism speaks directly to that Hegelian conundrum of the cunning of reason, whereby reason tricks the passions into being its agents so that history proceeds by inexorable, theological design.[41] One could argue that it is in the complexities of this equation, written large in Schreber, that one finds the essence of heroism as history has defined it: a great man is one whose passions become a conduit for universal reason; the great man falls – becomes 'mad' – when the desiring-flow shifts its course and reason becomes a conduit for passion. This equation accommodates the possibilities both of personal and of societal madness, depending on the historian's perspective, for the hero might be seen to have fallen from being a hero into being a

---

[41] See Collingwood, *The Idea of History*, 116–17, on this paradox.

madman, or the society might, in repudiating its hero, be seen as having proven itself mad; moreover, there is always room for the paradox that much madness is actually divinest sense (*Titus Andronicus*, maligned but, as is usual with Shakespeare, unimpeachably insightful, provides a reading text for the complexities of this reciprocal relationship, *As I Lay Dying* provides another). If history's preoccupation with heroism's systemic flux has the smell of inevitability about it, it is because this is yet another performance of historiography's Oedipal equilibrations; in its negotiation between desire and rectitude, and in its performative affiliations with the rational and the controlled over the desirous and the anarchic, it declares one more time its filial obeisance to the dangerous father. Selling Schreber down the Oedipal river: this is an emblematic gesture for a discipline whose preoccupation is with heroes and whose procedures, therefore, are themselves Oedipal, or vice versa.

The hero, history's darling, is defined by his precarious status just as history is configured in rises and falls; the shifting of the flow, the muddying of the semantic water so that reason and passion are no longer clearly distinguishable, transforms hero into madman. When the energy that has served a forseeably positive institutional or political end becomes deflected into the inexplicable, one says that the cunning of passion has taken over; this systemic equilibration, elegantly tautological, is endlessly recuperative of history – the subject and the discipline – as something whose essence is a rationality within which, and against which, both the alpine peaks of heroism and the excrudescences of the irrational stand. This affords history a sublime topography, but one safely considered within the level discursive terrain of the rational. Schreber's *Memoirs* is a profound relief in the consideration of heroes, for, just as it mends history's vexed relation with metaphysics by locating truth at once within and external to the material evidence, it also distills heroism into that condition of mad sanity about which, elsewhere, outside the asylum, it is so difficult to speak without equivocation. To contain Schreber's *Memoirs* within the disciplined rationalities of psychoanalysis and historiography is to face down the father-hero, to recognize the suffering, and the terrible risk one takes in speaking one's truth, but to do so without exiting the safety of the Oedipal nest. To contain 'history' – indeed, to *define* history – within these same disciplined rationalities and these formalized constraints is to face and also to face down the father-hero and to enforce the perpetual generation of duty-bound, castration-anxious competitors. The book of Schreber, read within the canonical discourse of this rationality, allows one to perform historiography's obligation to recognize but not recapitulate the sublime, to speak of heroes, to come to know them, without arrogating to itself the heroism it bespeaks.

This – this impulse to recognize but not recapitulate the sublime, to speak of heroes without arrogating to oneself, through a poetics of the sublime, the heroic stance – at once marks historiography's recognition of its Oedipal duty and its necessary, preordained resistance to that duty. The psychoanalytic, psychobiographical, and historiographical assessments of Schreber's *Memoirs* are subtle variations on this theme, as they incorporate Schreber's complex testimony into a system that, in sustaining the presence of that testimony, also enforces the will of the father as it is perceived in Oedipal terms. By controlling the reception of an otherwise anarchic and dangerously gender-bent text, these assessments not only write history but make it as well; they as much as guarantee history's future, for through the relentless *telos* of the Oedipal story, they keep the inexplicable, the ahistorical, and the 'feminine' at bay. By retrieving and endlessly chewing over the literal story of Schreber, father and son (and every retriever, sent out, comes in trailing a boot, a strap, a halter, some Schreberism entailed by the father on his son), they keep filial piety and paternal authority in place. Reading about Schreber, one cannot forget the paradox upon which history's preoccupation with great men is founded: to document and to analyze the sublimities of heroism is an act of homage that, while it performs history's obligation to humanize, performs as well an assimilative and recuperative gesture. The very language of historiography refutes the heroic stories it tells; it is a Scheherazadic defense against being lopped off in mid-story, as it walks the Oedipal line between admiration and competitive bravado, between an unabashed poetics and a dutiful reportage, and between the son's hero-worship and the father's heroic autonomy.

4

❖❖❖

Telling stories: historiography and narrative

❖❖❖

I placed a jar in Tennessee,
And round it was, upon a hill.
It made the slovenly wilderness
Surround that hill.

The wilderness rose up to it,
And sprawled around, no longer wild.
The jar was round upon the ground
And tall and of a port in air.

It took dominion everywhere.
The jar was gray and bare.
It did not give of bird or bush,
Like nothing else in Tennessee.

Wallace Stevens, 'Anecdote of the Jar'

As works of imagination, the historian's work and the novelist's do not differ. Where they do differ is that the historian's picture is meant to be true.   R. G. Collingwood, *The Idea of History*[1]

Ordinary Language

Historians are mostly inclined to write in plain, non-technical language that, as Marianne Moore would say, ordinary dogs and cats can read. Or, as Barzun says, the historian is committed to the language of butchers and bakers, for 'It is they – bakers, butchers, and historians – who set the standard. Barring an occasional need to employ the jargon of a trade or profession (shipping, war, coinage), the historian uses no language but that which will bring his narrative within the literate man's capacity to follow.'[2] In

---

[1] R. G. Collingwood, *The Idea of History*, ed. Jan Van Der Dussen (Oxford University Press, 1993), 246.

[2] Jacques Barzun, *Clio and the Doctors* (University of Chicago Press, 1974), 73–74. See, too for example, Paul K. Conkin and Roland N. Stromberg, *The Heritage and Challenge of History* (New York: Dodd, Mead, and Company, 1971), 246.

upholding the model of a language cleared of too many metaphors, purged of technical language, straightened from its natural predisposition for the turns to which tropology gives so many names, ballasted by material detail and freed of theoretical presumption, made, in short, to be both narratively accessible and immediately and plainly clear, the historian implies that he opts for a manly mutuality between speaker and hearer, author and reader. In promoting narrative as the most natural expression of history, he implies his immense confidence in a shared master plot. It is indeed a pact among literate men.

'The literate man' ('hypocrite lecteur! – mon semblable – mon frère!'): this is a code that speaks an entire Oedipal history. It sets the terms within parameters only apparently generous since the literate man has established his hegemony on premises of necessary exclusion. The historian's language choice is felt to keep things among hardworking, commonsensical, similarly educated men who may be counted upon to react in friendly or not so friendly, oedipalized, competition. The phantasmatic audience for conventional history-writing is male, and it is male of the most traditional and classically oedipalized sort: which is to say that it precludes sissies, effete intellectuals, and all such fancy talkers and momma's boys on the one hand, and a entire menagerie of variously incapacitated others – slaves, madmen, children, women – on the other. Queensbury rules apply, although the Oedipal impulse to clear the road of competition sometimes prevails, and the terms of the language game are precisely those which simultaneously authorize, legitimize, and necessitate Oedipal expectations. The game proceeds by the assumption that there is sharable wisdom of a worldly and useful sort, that it must be taught, that it is at once an obligation, a privilege, and at times a burden to speak the plain language of truth: this is Oedipal pedagogy, necessary explication of the sphinx's riddle, that phallic anxiety fable of erection into manhood and the fall into senescence, the beginning, the middle, and the end.

The conventional historian thus effects to speak in the pragmatic but unassuming language of the thoughtful journeyman who explicitly or implicitly dismisses overly refined, overly theoretized anxieties as outside his province; meticulously competent with the ruler and the level, he makes no claim beyond the practical, he is no mathematician playing cerebral games. Marc

Bloch's statement in *The Historian's Craft* is typical at the level of assertion, tone, and tactical modesty of historians' claims relative to what they suggest are more sophisticated or cerebral modes of discourse:

It is fitting that these few words of introduction be concluded with a confession . . . in order to understand and appreciate one's own methods of investigation . . . it is indispensable to see their connection with all simultaneous tendencies in other fields. Now this study of methods for their own sake is, in its turn, a specialized trade, whose technicians are called philosophers. That is a title to which I cannot pretend. Through this gap in my education this essay will doubtless lose much in both precision of language and breadth of horizon. I submit it for what it is and no more: the memorandum of a craftsman who has always liked to reflect over his daily task, the notebook of a journeyman who has long handled the ruler and the level, without imaging himself to be a mathematician.[3]

The terms of this resistance to theory are predicated on a manly, if oedipalized ambivalence that refuses to yield to inner doubt or externally imposed authority even as these forces are acknowledged through maneuvers like self-irony and a rather proud deprecation about being a 'mere historian.' The curiously defensive apologias of historians writing about historiography (as opposed to writing history) are in keeping with this claim of modest practicality; they are fraught with the ambivalence of one who sees his primary disciplinary imperatives threatened by the very attempt to philosophize. 'What is history?' asks Carr, 'I have no fear that my subject may, on closer inspection seem trivial. I am afraid only that I may seem presumptuous to have broached a question so vast and so important' (Carr had done better to fear the first charge, since Gay, in *Freud for Historians*, calls his book 'widely read, resolutely trivial').[4]

This commitment to a simple language unburdened with rhetorical, philosophical, technical, or poetic complexity enacts itself within an already elaborated fiction, arguing the quiet confidence of the 'ordinary' man who speaks it, its reticence is fully encoded within a world of stories and character types. Bloch's description of himself, for example, echoes the figure of the worker-savant of the nineteenth-century realistic novel, a fantasy which in its turn

[3] Marc Bloch, *The Historian's Craft*, trans. Peter Putnam (New York: Vintage Books, 1953), 19.

[4] Edward Hallett Carr, *What is History?* (New York: Alfred A. Knopf, 1962), 5. Peter Gay, *Freud for Historians* (Oxford University Press, 1985), 8.

echoes entire story-books of admirably laconic men. In *Mary Barton*, Elizabeth Gaskell describes the factory hand and entomologist, Job Legh. 'There is a class of men in Manchester,' she begins, and all over the manufacturing districts, who think, read, and study without the least degree of pretension, 'weavers, common hand-loom weavers, who throw the shuttle with unceasing sound, though Newton's "Principia" lies open on the loom, to be snatched at in work hours, but revelled over in meal times or at night . . . It is perhaps less astonishing that the more popularly interesting branches of natural history have their warm and devoted followers among this class. There are botanists . . . There are entomologists.'[5] Hands-on experts, workers, these men the 'natural' intellectuals who need nothing fancy in the way of education, jargon, or equipment; they are so intrinsically sufficient that dressed-up language would be superfluous. The historian, a sort of pastoral model of this worker-savant, may aspire to a plainness of language as simple, and as elegantly complex, as an egg.

And in the spirit of communicational charity, one might very well provisionally agree that sometimes plain talk is best, that as a general principle of polite conversation, such apparent diffidence may promote more volubility if less precision than the rigorously deployed language of high theory or philosophy or psychoanalysis. Bertrand Russell, one feels, is only speaking for the common-sensical brotherhood when he says that immunity from eloquence is vital to the citizens of a democracy. And indeed, often this hope for a less tropological language backs a commendable effort to speak as honestly, responsibly, and clearly as one can, an effort that can be opposed to the conscious use of a language whose rhetorical tactics are irresponsible or resolutely biased, designed, as a lawyer's summation might be designed, to produce the desired verdict by demagogic means. While it could be truly said that neither product is metaphor-free, pragmatically there may be a real difference between the two attempts. Putting aside all questions of metahistory, bracketing the conviction that one can, as does Hayden White, speak of a 'poetics of history,' one can still make useful, small distinctions having to do with clarity, purpose, tone, and pedagogical and performative effect.[6]

[5] Elizabeth Gaskell, *Mary Barton* (Oxford University Press, 1987), 40–41 (chapter 5).
[6] Hayden White, *Metahistory: The Historical Imagination in Nineteenth-Century Europe* (Baltimore: Johns Hopkins, 1973).

Yet, ironically, this righteous fantasy of completely straightforward language all too easily itself degenerates into what White, in his 1976 essay 'Rhetoric and History,' calls the 'rhetoric of anti-rhetoric.'[7] Contemporary historians of the self-defined 'old-fashioned' school may unembarrassedly turn to rhetorically lively, metaphor laden prose in what they have come to feel as a genuine war against historiographic irresponsibilities. G. R. Elton's *Return to Essentials*, for example, generally works at the double level of open attack and innuendo, and if rhetorical finesse is to some extent a product of its genre (the public/academic lecture), its spleen is nonetheless given remarkably unreserved play in flamboyant language. He speaks a full rhetorical range of anti-rhetoric, from Swiftian irony to invective. He speaks of Hayden White, for example, who 'having produced various modest works in the history of ideas,' then presumed to write more, or of David Harlan, who writes an article about intellectual history for the *American Historical Review* and who has also (and by implication only) 'published one short study of the American clergy in the eighteenth century.' Theory is 'German philosophy and French *esprit* – a dangerous cocktail because while the former may be incomprehensible it looks wise, and the latter demonstrates that the absurd always sound better in French.' 'Fanatical feminists' attempt 'to marry deconstruction and Marxism, which is like spiking vodka with LSD.' Elton performs the historian's point: that unfettered rhetorical play can be virtually irresistible at the moments of its utterance. He laments French theory as 'a discourse . . . in which metaphors regularly do duty for rational thinking,' and it is only after the fact that one remembers that this is the pot calling the kettle black.[8]

The fantasy of plain talk, plain thought, plain work, plain ideas also writes itself against an already-elaborated background; among likeminded people acquainted with the human condition, a great deal may remain unsaid and still be heard; from within solidarity, simplicity speaks worlds; inside solidarity there is safety from all the barbarians of theory, feminism, etc.; likemindedness repudiates by its very form the unwanted outsiders and the

---

[7] Hayden White, 'Rhetoric and History,' in *Theories of History* (Los Angeles: Williams Andrews Clark Memorial Library, 1976), 10.

[8] G. R. Elton, *Return to Essentials* (Cambridge University Press, 1991), 28, 29, 29, 37.

misshapen parvenjus of enlightenment. One thinks of Franken-stein's monster who, hiding in a pigsty, learns to speak and read – indeed, who comes into consciousness – through a series of purely canonical texts but who cannot, nonetheless, for the life of him join the party inside. Or of the old joke of the new prison inmate baffled as the oldtimers occasionally shout out a number, at which everyone laughs; the jokes, he discovers, have been told so many times that they may be communicated numerically yet in full ribald force to initiates. This tacit agreement to ordinariness or laconic reserve only suffices, however, within a group who already share a great deal, and, of equal importance, it only suffices for one validated before the fact as a legitimate participant in the conversation (one may very well *share*, as does Franken-stein's monster, the curriculum, the language, and the philosophy of the status quo and still be excluded from the discussions; the new inmate who shouts out a correct number will generate hostility rather than laughter, for entering the discourse without first having become licensed to do so). As I have said elsewhere, some of us might feel like Alice at the Hatter's tea-party: ' "Take some more tea," the March Hare said to Alice very earnestly. "I've had nothing yet," Alice replied in an offended tone: "so I can't take more." "You mean you can't take *less*," said the Hatter: "it's very easy to take *more* than nothing." '[9]

In other words, it is all very well and good within a brotherhood to 'speak no language but that which will bring ... narrative within the literate man's capacity to follow,' all very well and good among the brotherhood to proceed as if its narratives were patterned from the shape and sound of reality itself, and as if, following from that Cinderella story of the shoe fitting, such language deployed narrativistically represented the *sine qua non* of communicational competence. Who can complain, after all, about being called to the reasonableness of the 'literate man,' human-ism's domestication of a potentially more sharp-edged, stateless, unpredictable, and unaffiliated intelligence? As Barzun says, the butcher, the baker, and the historian, those three men in a tub, sum up the appropriate voice from which plain, practical talk should emanate; if history is a 'slaughter bench' it is nonetheless produc-

---

[9] Lewis Carroll, Alice's Adventures in Wonderland & Through the Looking Glass (New York: Clarkson N. Potter, Inc., 1960), 70.

tive of a meat and potatoes ethos.[10] Who can complain but those who fail to fit the terms and thus prove themselves before the fact either as *too* intellectual to care about material specifics historically displayed (philosophers, theoreticians, psychoanalysts) or, at the other end of the spectrum, as *un*reasonable and, by extension, inhuman (women, children, madmen, etc.). The historian typically justifies his strong commitment to good, plain narrative by evoking a sort of populist utopia – butchers, bakers, historians, surveyors, carpenters, guild-workers of various types – where modest common sense and a common curriculum prevails and nobody has to get hung up on fancy words like 'reify' and 'overdetermined' and 'cathexis.' It seems, by definition, so unpretentious and hardworking and representative a group as to discredit through the sheer fact of its reasonableness those who question its working premises or who exceed or fail to meet its terms.

But in fact, from a theoretical point of view this reliance upon common narrative in simple language appears only an apparent modesty and far from simple in its motivation; it seems anything but an admission of the contingencies of audience expectation, anything but a tacit acknowledgement that one's history-telling is vulnerable to the anamorphoses of one's own insights, blindnesses, and obsessions; it seems, in fact, a marvelous effrontery that suggests, not diffidence in the face of uncertainty, not Habermasian inclinations toward enhancing communication, but the quiet confidence of the faithful (one must distinguish here between the enactment of narrative in history-writing and the more defensive statements regarding narrative one finds in statements on historiographic principles). Joan Scott says of this kind of historical knowing, 'The form that knowledge has taken – the remarkable absence or subordination of women in the narratives of the 'rise of civilization,' their particularity in relation to Universal Man, their confinement to studies of the domestic and private – indicates a politics that sets and enforces priorities, represses some subjects in the name of the greater importance of others, naturalizes certain categories and disqualifies others.'[11]

[10] For Hegel's reference to history as 'slaughter bench,' see Dominick LaCapra, 'The Temporality of Rhetoric,' in *Chronotypes: The Construction of Time*, eds. John Bender and David E. Wellbery (Stanford University Press, 1991), 124.

[11] Joan W. Scott, *Gender and the Politics of History* (New York: Columbia University Press, 1988), 9.

The old, old story, with all the weight of history behind it, has more than its considerable inertia to keep it going; genealogically impressive – it *is* history, after all – it rebukes upstarts and newcomers with a sense that taste dictates a certain quiet fidelity to its unwritten and unspoken terms.

Implicit in historiography's defense of honest story-telling is the (threatened) conviction that one's audience shares a prior reality whose most basic terms are not just set, but sufficient. Lyotard speaks in *The Postmodern Condition* of 'the preeminence of the narrative form in the formulation of traditional knowledge'; 'Narration,' he says, 'is the quintessential form of customary knowledge, in more ways than one.'[12] The historian, whose aspirations are toward truth, implies through his preference for story-telling that he tolerates the apparently contingent aspects of narrative construction precisely *because* he retains his bedrock faith that material evidence will fall into its natural place within the already-written truth. Peter Novick's introduction to *That Noble Dream*, which has spoken to justify its length of 632 pages, concludes, 'The plot of this book is easily summarized,' 'Although the story can be easily summarized, it cannot be quickly or easily told.'[13] This is the paradox on which such assumptions must rest: that 632 pages of meticulously annotated and detailed evidence is utterly necessary and, at the same time, multiplicative elaborations on one easily summarized story. A madman/hermaphrodite like Schreber must employ all the weapons of argumentative rhetoric in the hopes of winning inclusion into this charmed circle of story-tellers, but he fails to understand that the proof of a successfully oedipalized manliness is in the *performance*, narrative, political, sexual, and otherwise. To talk the talk is to walk the walk.

The historian's choice of narrative, presented with a kind of Will Rogers irony as simple homeliness in a world of academic philosophers and other Laputans, stands as proof that he has successfully negotiated the Oedipal contract into manhood; the good narrative will perform at the level of productive normalcy regardless of the subject or pathology it treats; it will assimilate and democratize, bringing even the most resistant theoretical

[12] Jean-François Lyotard, *The Postmodern Condition: A Report on Knowledge*, trans. Geoff Bennington and Brian Massumi (Minneapolis: University of Minnesota Press, 1988), 19.

[13] Peter Novick, *That Noble Dream: The 'Objectivity Question' and the American Historical Profession* (Cambridge University Press, 1988), 15, 17.

systems down to earth. 'Success through common speech illus-trates a principle,' says Barzun, 'in order to be of use to the historian, psychological as well as other technical terms must first fall into the public domain. It has always been so.'[14] 'Historians have, for the best of reasons, rejected a highly technical vocabulary or jargon,' say Conkin and Stromberg, 'Such a vocabulary, even though originally a shortcut to clarity, almost always ossifies and, in vulgar form, becomes the favorite camouflage of mindlessness and mediocrity.'[15] Hayden White points out in 'Narrativity in the Representation of Reality' that real events, that is 'events . . . offered as the proper content of historical discourse, are real

not because they occurred but because, first, they were remembered and, second, they are capable of finding a place in a chronologically ordered sequence. In order, however, for an account of them to be considered a historical account, it is not enough that they be recorded in the order of their original occurrence. *It is the fact that they can be recorded otherwise, in an order of narrative, that makes them, at one and the same time, questionable as to their authenticity and susceptible to being considered as tokens of reality.*[16]

Yet for traditional historiography this paradox can by definition have little force as a theoretical issue, for a plain and unpretentious narrativity declares and creates and teaches Oedipal authority: the full oxymoronic implications of this narrative gambit can only be heard from outside the expectations that generate it; from within it is the dare that one takes to prove one's membership in the club.

The implicit self-satisfaction of narrative has, of course, pushed many historians into ascetic resolve; in the arc of the pendulum's swing, there is a place to designate the several moments over time at which the pleasures of narrative have come to seem untoward. Benjamin sees historical materialism as a resistance to the beguil-ing force of story-telling, its own desires more fruitfully spent in the manly task of iconoclasm: 'The historical materialist,' he says, 'leaves it to others to be drained by the whore called "Once upon a time" in historicism's bordello. He remains in control of his power, man enough to blast open the continuum of history.'[17] The modernist literary intuition that ordinary, old-fashioned narrative

[14] Barzun, *Clio and the Doctors*, 73.
[15] Conkin and Stromberg, *The Heritage and Challenge of History*, 246.
[16] Hayden White, *The Content of the Form* (Baltimore: Johns Hopkins University Press, 1978), 20. Italics mine.
[17] Walter Benjamin, *Illuminations: Essays and Reflections*, ed. Hannah Arendt, trans. Harry Zohn (New York: Schocken Books, 1968), 262.

is insufficient to a full expression of anxiety, disorientation, anguish, ennui, arousal, impotence, etc. often translates itself in direct proportion to historical horrors. For many historians of the Holocaust, story-telling is part and parcel of the 'historicism' that ameliorates the unspeakable: 'Historicism,' says Sande Cohen, is 'an attempt to achieve a cultural "timeless time," an image which holds together categories such as origin and result. Historicism . . . renders an image of an unavoidable presentation handed down by "history" which braids past, present, and future in the here and now. One is at once anchored to both a date and an image; one starts one's narration by setting the clock at a metaphoric midnight – time "counts" because the historian imputes this clock to the events recounted. (There are restorative countings, apocalyptic ones, and so on.)'[18]

In the choice between what he reads as Habermas' move toward a Hegelian–Freudian synthesis and what he sees as Lyotard's more anarchic desire, Cohen would choose Lyotard, and the anti-Oedipal possibilities of 'dispossession': '*Dispossession* has a number of senses, but it commonly refers to events which prevent consciousness from being the subject of traditions, disciplines, and interpretation. The disseizure through insight, a person's refusal to agree with an oedipalizing evaluation, a painting's ability to frustrate one's subjective expectations, the momentary appearance of the sublime, are examples of dispossession.'[19] Both Cohen and Lyotard view the oedipalized artifact as soothing one into modes of identification with the already-written; one falls possessed into the embrace of history. In Adorno's words, the value of dispossession is that it is 'no longer a message, threat, beseechment, defense, exorcism, lesson or allusion in a symbolic relation, but rather an absolute object, delivered of transferential relation, indifferent to the order of relations, active only in the order of energies, in the silence of the body.' It is, in other words, outside of history, because it has escaped that 'whore called "once upon a time."'[20] Narrative's teleological lullabies are, in these formulations, to be resisted in order that true 'history' may be freed from its encasement in the continuum of history into full, potent being.

---

[18] Sande Cohen, 'Between Image and Phrase: Progressive History and the 'Final Solution' as Dispossession,' in *Probing the Limits of Representation: Nazism and the Final Solution* (Cambridge, Mass.: Harvard University Press, 1992), 171. See too Sande Cohen, *Historical Culture: On the Decoding of an Academic Discipline* (Berkeley: University of California, 1986). [19] *Ibid.*, 177. [20] *Ibid.*, 178.

And indeed, the conventional historian's reliance upon narrative suggests that within oedipalized discourse discrete historical events are felt chronotopically: that they are apprehended as doubly and inextricably invested in time and space because within the fated progress of the Oedipal journey, every move is fraught with historic, spatio-temporal inevitability. Thus the wager that 'true' historical details will be imbued with enough chronotopic force to accommodate all reasonable narrative interventions and rearrangements, that, in fact, they will rise to the challenge narrative offers to simple chronology and thus *prove* themselves authentic tokens of reality. Bloch distinguishes the rich medium of 'historical time' from that which may be chopped 'up into arbitrarily homogenous segments' by those for whom 'time is nothing more than a measurement.'

In contrast, historical time is a concrete and living reality with an irreversible onward rush. It is the very plasma in which events are immersed, and the field within which they become intelligible.[21]

The backbone of conventional historiography is this fully re-ticulated and meaningful materialized time, onto which the circumstantial elaborations of history will superimpose themselves by a kind of natural accretion, and even the historian's own place *within* time, history, and the contingencies of culture and circumstance will be equilibrated within this system. Historical time, felt and expressed metonymously, will declare itself through the contiguous flow from the historian's pen. And another way of putting it is this: historical time felt as 'plasma,' returned through the narrative flow to plasma, is a healing infusion for the Oedipally anxious historian, a way of sustaining both a sense of continuity and of contiguity with one's own past and of mitigating the needful fantasy/fear of castration. At the heart of this procedural preference for narrative is a fantasy of absolute translation of the Oedipal contract: the historian as medium, neither hysterically prophetic nor inspirationally hyperbolic – not Schreberian, not poetic, but *medium* in every sense of the word.

Indeed, the historian's insistence upon his narrative as sufficient to truthtelling, as distinguishable from fiction, and as divested of 'the vividly felt portion of [the past] that involves one's own life' suggests a virtually Platonic or theocratic faith; it is as if to say that

[21] Bloch, *The Historian's Craft*, 27–28.

historical realness, with its evidential base, is backed by ideal forms whose potency will override even the fictionalizing energies of story-telling.[22] As White says, 'It is historians themselves who have transformed narrativity from a manner of speaking into a paradigm of the form that reality itself displays to a "realistic" consciousness. It is they who have made narrativity into a value, the presence of which in a discourse having to do with "real" events signals at once its objectivity, its seriousness, and its realism.'[23] This valorizing of narrative stands as a gesture of wish fulfillment; promoted as a way of articulating reality through a realistic consciousness, it lays claims both to a deep ontological normalcy and to the virtually speaking power of material circumstance. It lays claim, in other words to itself, to History, for good narrative is precisely that narrative through which the vatic may speak – history prophesying its repetitions and thus predicting and effecting the future. Thus one senses that within the historiographic preoccupation with the question of who may speak and how exactly one *may* speak resides the conviction that one must be a true initiate, rather than some poor, monomaniacal Schreber whose visitations are not real but hallucinatory. Schreber, who keeps losing organs (his stomach, for example, periodically disappears, or his penis), whose intuitions of temporal and spatial contiguity are too voraciously comprehensive (as he sees his roommate 'becoming one with his bed,' so he feels himself eliding through physical states between maleness and femaleness; he is either eternal and immortal or subject to complete erasure – 'soul murder'), is a perfect model for Oedipal propaganda. Whether he is, as Freud says, a casualty of the father complex, or evidence of its status as linguistically, metaphorically, and symbolically overdetermined, Schreber remains a cautionary figure of what might happen when true prophetic channels are diverted by too much of the divided self.

The choice of narrative implies that behind the vicissitudes of every narrative there are a set of *a priori* values – regarding time and materiality – that will emerge naturally from the 'natural' mode of narration. The conventional historian's vocal and indignant rejection of 'unnatural' methods of narrativity (modernist experimentation as against realist linearity) and of elaborated or

[22] Barzun, *Clio and the Doctors*, 86.   [23] White, *The Content of the Form*, 24.

theoretical or technical language carries within it this faith in an exudant and normative normalcy. The historian's valorizing of narrative is not, as it might appear, based on a thin, graphically and diagrammatically unilateral vision, in which the syntagmatic energies of storytelling promote a linear vision of time; carried out as a gesture of solidarity, a testament of (now-shaken) faith, and a pedagogical responsibility to Oedipal teaching, it is, on the contrary, a dream of sufficiency. It is a (disguised) fulfillment of a (repressed) wish to reproduce history as full bodied, to keep it within the terms of the discipline as it was formally explicated and shaped in the nineteenth century: 'to make of history not merely a source of examples and a road to wisdom but a purposive force pregnant with the determinate destiny of man.'[24] This is not to say that the narrative can actually be made to transcend linearities, but that it is carried out under a fantasy of ripe tumescence. To be 'pregnant with the determinate destiny of man,' to be all-sufficient, hermaphroditically complete, would be to bring time and space together into one flesh: History.

Yet the historian would do well to take as emblematic Barthes' reading of Balzac's 'Sarrasine,' which in the context of a discussion of oedipalized expectations is more than ordinarily provocative. Balzac tells the story of the artist Sarrasine and his love for Zambinella, the beautiful singer whose gender Sarrasine discovers unequivocally through all the appropriate syllogisms ('I love her, therefore she is a woman,' 'She is weak, therefore she is a woman,' 'Beauty is the province of women and she is beautiful, therefore she is a woman'), and which he clinches most unarguably through his own question to her, 'Do you think you can deceive an artist's eye?'[25] That Zambinella has a penis clarifies matters painfully for Sarrasine, even if it only adds to the complexity for the rest of us, but Barthes' point is well taken nonetheless: 'the 'realistic' artist never places 'reality' at the origin of his discourse,' he says, 'but only and always, as far back as can be traced, an already written real, a prospective code, along which we discern, as far as the eye can see, only a succession of copies.'[26] The historian's faith in the plain language of the real shares this linguistic and allusively dense field of the already written real,

[24] Conkin and Stromberg, *The Heritage and Challenge of History*, 57.
[25] Roland Barthes, *S/Z*, trans. Richard Miller (New York: Hill and Wang, 1974), 247.
[26] *Ibid.*, 167.

which more often than not has such an inertial energy that its status as illusion is lost to its weighty, performative strength; it works as well within a more literally 'already written real' in that it includes among its evidential sources prior historical narratives; and it is, moreover, bound to the terms of the Oedipal contract which says that it must conduct its revisions from within an appropriate reverence for the past. What the historian takes as the 'paradigm of the form that reality itself displays to a "realistic" consciousness' may indeed be proceeding inexorably toward a revelation to which the circumstantial details lend their force, but its inevitabilities may come from influences other than the 'real.' Multiply overdetermined toward sustaining the past, linguistically as well as otherwise, conventional historiography is so inextricably united with the already written as to make its progress, like Oedipus' journey, always a movement back toward home.

In fact, knowing the considerable dangers of ignorance in this regard, the Oedipal merit badge system includes a genealogical component whereby one learns one's antecedents; acceptance of Oedipal rules automatically invokes kinship – to other men, texts, philosophies, pasts – as the first premise of an always incomplete and ambivalent repudiation of kinship. One can be neither a (good) philosopher nor an historian without communicating substantial evidence that one's present position is thoroughly contextualized, won through hard engagement with past authority. And because history *is* the past it can never win its way out of a maze of legitimating footnotes and tangible evidence into a new conceptual scheme. The historian working within language and history cannot entertain the Cartesian fantasy of a pure rational intelligence that, rejecting the past, builds from the ground up: 'The greatest advantage I derived from the study [of the manners of other men],' says Descartes, 'consisted in this, that, observing many things which, however extravagant and ridiculous to our apprehension, are yet by common consent received and approved by other great nations, I learned to entertain too decided a belief in regard to nothing of the truth of which I had been persuaded merely by example and custom; and thus I gradually extricated myself from many errors powerful enough to darken our natural intelligence, and incapacitate us in great measure from listening to reason.' By Cartesian definition, a discourse on such a method as he advocates will not *teach* the method but only describe it, for one who only follows another's lead betrays the iconoclasm central to the Cartesian premise of investigation: 'This tract,' says Descartes of the *Discourse*, 'is put forth merely as a history, or, if you will, as a tale, in which, amid some examples worthy of imitation, there will be found, perhaps, as many more which it were advisable not to follow.'[27] To *do* is to make history, to talk about having done is to write it.

The fantasy of complete individuation – of separating oneself entirely from the flow of time and history – is likely to be only that, a fantasy, as long as one is articulating oneself within language; but it is nonetheless central to western thought. The canonical call to arms, one that has been echoed from Aristotle to Montaigne to Heidegger, is this: 'Oh, my friends, there is no friend.' As Derrida points out in 'The Politics of Friendship,' this lament is a paradox that can only be enacted within the brotherhood; there is something quintessentially Oedipal in it, as it embodies in a single oxymoronic construction – 'Oh, my friends, there is no friend' – the dual imperatives of the Oedipal contract: at once to challenge and reaffirm the authority of kinship, to remain within the family circle by initializing its authority through realigned allegiances with it, to ingratiate and exasperate simultaneously, to embrace the freedom of the friendless condition by invoking one's autonomy among friends. To be able to say, in short, 'Oh, my friends, there is no friend.' Philosophy can well entertain this paradox, for the hallmark of a great philosopher (as distinguished from one who proves, by working within the given paradigms of his speciality, that he is rather an historian of philosophy) is exactly this triumph of idiosyncratic universality over traditional expectation; the hallmark of a philosophical genius (or a poet) would be one who could make complete newness authoritative in and of itself, rather than situating it against (and within) the repudiated past.[28] But a great historian will be great by virtue of his vatic translation of past into present. He must simultaneously preserve

---

[27] René Descartes, *A Discourse on Method, Meditations on the First Philosophy, Principles of Philosophy*, trans. John Veitch (London: J. M. Dent, 1994), 6, 4.

[28] For essays that pursue the implications of thinking in terms of a 'history of philosophy,' and that enrich the question of a 'philosophy of history,' see *Philosophy in History: Essays on the Historiography of Philosophy*, ed. Richard Rorty, J. B. Schneewind, Quentin Skinner (New York: Cambridge University Press, 1993).

and reinvent, conserve and spend the tokens of the past; he must embrace and reject the brotherhood of historians. History, like philosophy, is a discourse based on what Derrida defines as 'a friendship prior to friendships, an ineffaceable, fundamental, and bottomless friendship, one that draws its breath in the sharing of language . . . and in the being-together that any allocution supposes, including a declaration of war,' but its very substance restricts the terms of the negotiations.[29]

A friendship *that draws its breath in the sharing of language*: thus 'ordinary' talk, its terms already within the public domain, becomes both proof of kinship and the shared mode within which authority and influence may be disputed. Conventional historians' attitudes toward psychohistory enforce this point from within the discipline.[30] For the psychobiographer or psychohistorian who declares himself as such the effect is something like coming out of the closet as regards one's gender: he negotiates a treacherous path between activism and conciliation as he functions among historians who are generally felt as likely to be antipathetic to the enterprise. Gay, in assessing the Houses' book on Wilson, says, 'The tantalizing material they present might have permitted a more radical psychoanalytic reading than they have chosen to give it, but that would certainly have further increased the risk of rejection by the historical fraternity.' His own experience of causing a 'genteel riot' among historians because of a paper 'conventional in its method and presuppositions' and with 'very little psychoanalysis in it' is also telling: 'I felt like a witch doctor who, by some ghastly social gaffe, had been invited to address the meeting of a medical society.'[31]

But only one who is by definition excluded from kinship rights can know just how merciless this genealogically derived version of normalcy can be. The successfully oedipalized could not even *hear* the fully fraught complexity of Zambinella's plea to Sarrasine as s/he asks that the filial contract be expanded to a more comprehensive concept of brotherhood. Certainly, he would not be able to see, much less to write, her history or – even more provocative – the history of homophilia/phobia that makes such Schreberian

[29] Jacques Derrida, 'The Politics of Friendship,' *The Philosophical Forum*, 85, 636.
[30] See, for example, David Stannard, *Shrinking History: On Freud and the Failure of Psychohistory* (New York: Oxford University Press, 1980).
[31] Gay, *Freud For Historians*, 214, 13.

fantasies so deeply familiar (it is not only Zambinella whose need is fulfilled through transvestitism, but her male audience's as well). 'Ah, you would not love me as I long to be loved,' s/he says, and Sarrasine replies, 'How can you say that?' She answers:

Not to satisfy any vulgar passion; purely. I abhor men perhaps even more than I hate women. I need to seek refuge in friendship. For me the world is a desert. I am an accursed creature, condemned to understand happiness, to feel it, to desire it, and, like many others, forced to see it flee from me continually. Remember, sir, that I will not have deceived you. I forbid you to love me. I can be your devoted friend, for I admire your strength and your character. I need a brother, a protector. Be all that for me but no more.[32]

This is, of course, unhearable by Sarrasine, as it seems to come from a woman's mouth, and it is answered therefore with the two terms by which history consigns such speeches as Zambinella's to alternate meanings: 'My dearest angel,' he says, 'Coquette!' With Oedipal translator-machine in place, even the language of monsters, transvestites, women, and madmen can be read. But for the irrefutable fact of Zambinella's penis (what else, of course?), Sarrasine could have transcribed her indefinitely into the terms of his story. And even the penis fails to restore Zambinella's plea to any plausible and effective meaning (although it makes perfect sense) because, like Schreber, s/he is felt to move only between poles of monstrosity and madness. Statements of conventional historiographic method proselytize for normalcy, and they reify it, both to perpetuate its force and to minimize the 'risk of rejection by the historical fraternity.' A project carried out under more than usual duress, historiography's Oedipal negotiations for power generate rigorous rules of order.

Thus the standard indictment against literary realism – that despite its reformative expectations or its best intentions, it is doomed to reify the status quo and to act as an agent of control within it – may actually be more appropriate to historical narrative; certainly historiography's faith that a good historical narrative will, by virtue of its goodness, and as evidence of its goodness, shape itself to the terms of truth suggests that it considers certain truths inalienable. Barthes' assertion to the contrary, realist fiction, by virtue of its status as art and as fiction, resists at multiple levels

---

[32] Barthes, *S/Z*, 247.

the 'already written,' because its commitment to representational accuracy and to an extra-textual agenda (social reform, political or moral change, etc.) comes up against its equal commitment to performing *as fiction*. It is licensed to be teleologically inclined even as it also seeks to reproduce the indeterminacies of a less than ordered external reality. This conflictual field inevitably subverts the sort of automatic appropriations that Barthes implies are endemic to realism, destabilizing habitual gestures with tropological energies that throw prior discourses back on themselves. As I have argued elsewhere, the fictional truth within realism will necessarily be felt as precarious, tenuous, circumstantial, and contingent because it intentionally carries itself out in the oxymoronic space between history and poetry. Even the most programmatic of artistic theories of realism will be subverted at some level by the license, and the licentiousness, of the aesthetic pleasures of fictionalizing. But *history*, the historians hasten to say, is emphatically not fiction – 'the historian's picture,' says Collingwood, 'is meant to be true' – and the Althusserean argument that realist narrative is complicit with the status quo more nearly applies in this place where narrative must be disciplined into non-metaphoric, non-poetic truth-telling.[33] In popular narratives, says Lyotard, 'the speech acts relevant to this form of knowledge are performed not only by the speaker but also by the listener, as well as by the third party referred to. The knowledge arising from such an apparatus may seem 'condensed' in comparison with what I call 'developed' knowledge ... What is transmitted through these narratives is the set of pragmatic rules that constitutes the social bond.'[34] In history, the Oedipal question of who wears the penis in the family is asked in terms so formalized as to generate its own answers, and it operates within a linguistic and symbolic system so tightly enclosed that any phallic inconveniences may be retroactively explained away.

This is not to say, of course, that the historian's efforts to purge language of its more anarchic figurative content can be successful, as de Man's reading of Locke's rejection of elaboration in the *Essay Concerning Human Understanding* makes clear; nor is it to say that responsibility regarding rhetorical tactics is not necessary, commendable, and pragmatically effective; but it is only to say that the

[33] Collingwood, *The Idea of History*, 246.
[34] Lyotard, *The Postmodern Condition*, 21.

status of true narrative as a desideratum is significant evidence of the will to Oedipal power and proof of the necessity of Oedipal amnesia.[35] Locke's injunctions against figurative language speak directly to de Man's point that one cannot resist the cumulative tropological energies within persuasive discourse: 'If we would speak of things as they are, we must allow that all the art of rhetoric, besides order and clearness, all the artificial and figurative application of words eloquence hath invented, are for nothing else but to insinuate wrong ideas, move the passions, and thereby mislead the judgment, and so indeed are perfect cheats; and therefore, however laudable or allowable oratory may render them in harangues and popular addresses, they are certainly, in all discourses that pretend to inform or instruct, wholly to be avoided; and where truth and knowledge are concerned, cannot but be thought a great fault, either of the language or person that makes use of them.'[36] Looking for figurative language among historiographic warnings against figurative language is like shooting fish in a barrel because, of course, the metaphoricity at the heart of language makes certain, as Nietzsche has said, that truth will always be a mobile army of metaphors. The point is not, here, the truism that transparent language is impossible, but rather that the fantasy of judicious use, like the historian's embracing of narrative, is a necessary and a telling one.

The conventional historian's expectations for narrative are, in fact, semiotically and performatively complex, and his consistent advocacy of a language of simple, straightforward clarity thus may be felt to carry a significant and unacknowledged charge of negation. It is no surprise that the butcher, the baker, and the candlestick maker are not so prosaic a group as they pretend to be, but the no-nonsense Oedipal contract calls for productive action carried out in such a way as to enact and promote, as well as to enforce, manliness as normalcy (i.e., the status quo, i.e., sanity, i.e., power). And the Oedipal code of manliness is clearly set up against a series of antitheses which include introversion, changeableness, and undecidability. To reflect these effeminate qualities might be pleasurable – a truth the Schreber-text both asserts and performs – but it would not be responsible. To write a text that, by

---

[35] Paul de Man, 'The Epistemology of Metaphor,' *Critical Inquiry*, 5, 1 (1978), 13–30.
[36] John Locke, *An Essay Concerning Human Understanding*, Book 3, chapter 10, section 34.

virtue of its intricacies, enforces and indeed celebrates its own hermeneutic autonomy is something like a crime against history, and to *read* a text in these terms is to violate history as well. Thus the historian cries out against all such infiltrations, from literary theory, from psychoanalysis, from philosophy, that would supersede the illusion of the naturalness of history's emanations through and into narrative. Conventional historiography thus decries hermeneutic reading as the parallel sin to non-transparent writing, on the same grounds that it expresses its contempt for psychohistorical 'jargon.' Neither is felt to have a place within responsible oedipalized discourse.

Yet historiography is a critical enterprise and as such is committed to evaluative procedures regarding texts; it is very closely affiliated in this sense to literary analysis, despite the often vocal resistance of historians who wish to preserve the illusion of objectivity, clarity, simplicity, and good honest labor.[37] The negotiations are complex by which historians distance themselves from the double sense that evidence should be allowed to speak for itself and the sense that it *cannot*, after all, speak for itself without both the interpretive help and the critical engagement of the historian. Collingwood consistently argues that the 'scissors-and-paste' method which puts together authorities into a collage 'is not really history' because it fails at two levels: to be consciously and aggressively critical in its assessments of what constitutes authority and to be sufficiently aware that it can never actually proceed by the rules it sets for itself, since choices are always being made by the writer, evidence always being arranged.[38] Collingwood, of course, also dismisses 'critical history' simply perceived, for from his philosophical position one cannot absolutely verify the accuracy of authority in any event, even under rigorous methods, but he does not carry his skepticism to its logical conclusion: to think and proceed hermeneutically is also misguided. 'Now anyone,' says Collingwood, 'who has read Vico, or even a second-hand version of some of his ideas, must have known that the important question about any statement contained in a source is not whether it is true or false, but what it means.'[39] Elton, with his characteristic intemperance, goes further: 'Hermeneutics is the science which

---

[37] See, for example, Barzun's section called 'The Danger of Reading Signs,' 50–54, in *Clio and the Doctors*.   [38] Collingwood, *The Idea of History*, 257–59.

[39] *Ibid.*, 260 (see, too, p. 264).

invents meaning; historical study depends on discovering meaning without inventing it. Therefore, hermeneutics is a term not only not applicable to the historian's operation but positively hostile to it; its use enables the student to impose meaning on his materials instead of extracting meaning and import from them.'[40] The tactics of hermeneutic reading open a dangerous passageway into interpretation: in this method, 'if in some source you found a statement which for some reason could not be accepted as literally true, you must not on that account reject it as worthless. It might be a way, perhaps a well-established way according to the custom of the time when it was written, of saying something which you, through ignorance of that custom, did not recognize as its meaning.'[41] Such a text might, in other words, be felt to conduct itself symbolically, metaphorically, or cabalistically, and the historian would then be pulled into the treacherous world of signs and symbols. 'History,' the literally true, would be of no more and perhaps of even less significance than the not literally true, the metaphorical, or the euphemistic. The 'natural' order by which good narrative reveals historical truth would be disrupted, undermined by the opacities and convolutions of indeterminate or hermeneutically determined meaning. One could not, in this anxiety dream, *perform* one's Oedipal duty to distinguish between true and false, mad and sane, reasonable and unreasonable. If Oedipus had been able to read all of the signs, to discover the densely layered complexities of his fate, he might never have taken a step. Schreber's *Memoirs*, with its madman's impeccable logic and its oxymoronic condition as hallucinatory truth, is exactly the nightmare hyperbole by which this phobia may be measured, for if read without oedipalized temperance and analytic phrasebook in hand it threatens to proliferate into unbounded significance.

Yet repudiating what he sees as the overcompensations by which hermeneutic reading subsumes everything, whether factually or historically true or false, into 'meaning,' the historian himself must account for an activity that is essentially critical and interpretive in nature – what else does it mean to engage in 'extracting meaning and import' from materials? And even as he seeks to distance himself from the implications of reading and

[40] Elton, *Return to Essentials*, 30.   [41] Collingwood, *The Idea of History*, 259.

proceeding hermeneutically he insists upon working within narrative, with all its teleological predispositions, all its tendencies to feed upon its own language; protestations of simplicity seem, under the circumstances, more than ordinarily to function as gestures of denial. If Collingwood himself rejects Viconian assumptions, he offers an evaluative process of his own that has since become the source of almost cabalistic schools of interpretation.[42] Yet the historian typically decries what he feels to be the psychoanalytic or hermeneutic overinterpretation of evidence, indulgences conflated by Barzun in *Clio and the Doctors* as 'semeiology, the theory of signs and symptoms,' while he nonetheless conducts a semiological exercise of his own: as Barzun says, the historian's '"understanding" in both senses – that is, his intellect and what satisfies it – is governed by a far subtler use of words than the technical. The signs and intimations to which he responds are more numerous and free.'[43] It is a fine line to walk, this tightrope over the abyss of semiotics; 'As the tradition of text criticism shows,' says Barzun, balancing with his long pole in hand on the trembling wire, 'a long chain of plausible arguments seems to make up for its fragility by its virtuoso skill. It has the appeal of the detective's demonstration in the final chapter. But solid history can only regard such gymnastics as a curiosity. The historian suspects the chain of might-be's in which every weak link is a threat to truth. He wants not a chain but a network of cross-confirming testimony; for he is not deciphering a code, he is visualizing a scene and a story.'[44] Yet, as the historians themselves make clear, even 'solid history,' conducted by the 'mere historian' Barzun valorizes over the pretentious and the semiotically inclined, is an act of critical and interpretive skill: just as surely as they reject fancy language and metaphor using fancy language and metaphor, they reject all but the most straightforward of relationships with the interpretive process while employing the devices by which texts are evaluated and reconfigured critically.

Oedipal subversions

Conventional historiography's vested interest in projecting and promoting Oedipal normalcy is, paradoxically enough, perhaps

---

[42] See the editor's introduction to *The Idea of History*.
[43] Barzun, *Clio and the Doctors*, 53, 65.   [44] *Ibid.*, 97.

most unequivocally manifested in its antipathy toward psychohistoriographic methods; and psychohistoriography's own similar resistance is reified in its pronounced ambivalence toward the consistent deployment of technically precise psychoanalytic language. If hermeneutic readings may be felt to promote the extra-historical autonomy of texts, it is felt that psychohistoriographic readings of evidence necessarily compound these sins. In *Clio and the Doctors* Barzun attacks psychohistory as by definition invested in concealment and self-delusion on the one hand and overinterpretation and invention on the other; given to what he calls 'weasel words,' it opens itself to a world of unmanly sins: to evasion, cunning, and innuendo, to shape-shifting, cowardice, and behind-the-back calumny. He makes the standard assertion that metaphor must be seen for 'what it is,' and that under the best of circumstances it is not 'trustworthy'; the language of psychoanalysis, however, is a chimerical blend of the hermeneutic and analytic modes, a tangle of 'signs and symptoms.' 'The reader of metaphors cannot be expected to restrict his perception of likeness to the right feature of the things compared,' says Barzun. 'He may be on his guard as long as he sees metaphor for what it is, but in analytic language as in any other the image soon merges with its object, the analogy with the reality, at which point the problem of evidence reappears.'[45]

There is a distinctively Hawthornian flavor to this repudiation of psychohistorical interests, for it evokes the spectre of clandestine impulse awakened by the very mode of discourse into subversive power; a quintessentially Oedipal paranoia, it presumes a residual desire, awakened by the pan-sexuality of psychoanalysis, that would force a regression from manly straightforwardness into devious elaboration. If you walk deep enough into the woods, says Hawthorne, you find your human nature, desirous, covert, uncontrolled, uncivilized; things that once seemed simple become complex, and things that seemed complex become dangerously simple, and the balance between civil, moral, and familial duty and personal appetite threatens to shift. If you talk in psychoanalytic terms, says Barzun, you *perform* your own unmanning into the intrinsic deviousness of hermeneutic introspections, and you perform it in such a way as to be

---

[45] *Ibid.*, 47.

contaminative. The 'naturalness' by which historiographic narrative emerges as clear, powerful, and pure is in fact a naturalized artificiality, reflecting an Aristotelian balance of moderate virility: it is the 'natural' son Edgar in *King Lear*, the man who is in all things a mixture of independent strength and filial piety, rather than the 'natural' son, Edmund, the bastard freed by his blood to enormities of paternal abuse. Only among the naturally good will personal bias disclose itself candidly so that engagements are not covert but direct. As Barzun says:

> Bias also afflicts the ordinary historian, to be sure, but the safeguards against it are stronger, because the evidence to be sifted is in plain sight and the bias also. A writer may have political, religious, or esthetic prejudices that thwart his intellectual honesty; but they sooner or later disclose themselves, because he is not dealing in signs and metaphors. He can be challenged and asked to produce his sources, palpable, open to all.[46]

The tautological circle here is cast iron: if discourse is carried out in a manly (straightforward) way, it will emerge as manly – metaphors will, though unavoidable, declare themselves as such, and bias, though unavoidable, will declare itself as such; if discourse is carried out in an unmanly (non-straightforward) way, it will emerge as unmanly and be contaminative in its deviousness.

At first glance it would seem paradoxical that the very discourse, psychoanalysis, that provides the specifics of the Oedipal fantasy and that, in so doing, confirms its hegemony, would be the locus of such hostility among the successfully oedipalized. In fact, however, it communicates perfectly the first and most difficult rule of Oedipal procedure, which is that the proof is in the pudding. Real men don't *talk* about the difficulties of becoming, and remaining, successfully masculinized, but they *do* it. They are guildworkers, not intellectuals, practitioners, not theoreticians, historians, not novelists. Narrative – that most action-packed of modes – is a way of being manly even in the face of uncertainty; it is like riding into battle regardless of the fear at the pit of the stomach. As Barzun's title makes clear, history *is* narrative: *Clio and the Doctors: Psycho-history, Quanto-History, and History*. It holds the fort against an unmanly subjectivity, represented by the hermeneutical pseudo-science of psychoanalysis, and against the

---

[46] *Ibid.*, 48.

anti-humanist number-crunching of the statistician. Collingwood similarly and with biblical force impugns earlier, positivistic methods, 'Statistical research is for the historian a good servant but a bad master. It profits him nothing to make statistical generalizations, unless he can thereby detect the thought behind the facts about which he is generalizing.'[47] History is, as has been variously pointed out, his story, with *story* the locus of multiple significance and 'his' the token by which the manliness of the Oedipal contract may be claimed.

Neither Uriah Heepish implicatures nor dry-as-sticks statistics, only true historical narrative will perform the Oedipal trick of *being* rather than seeming, and thus conventional historiography's uneasiness in the face of all historiographic enterprises felt to threaten this performative potency. Psychohistory, quanto-history, post-structuralist and theoretically inclined history, philosophy of history, etc. all give up the laconically garrulous for the introspective and/or the metaphysical and/or inhuman, so that story-telling, outwardly directed and productive, yields to less performatively potent, more self-conscious modes. Psychoanalysis, not alone in being impugned by conventional historiography, arouses the most thoroughgoing defensiveness, and this not in spite of its Oedipal preoccupations but because of them. Psychoanalysis affords at once too much freedom, by virtue of its explicit license to analyze, to deconstruct, and to problematize the actions of men in time, and too little freedom: it is itself an enclosed system which reifies what are felt to be its own internal deterministic prejudices and whose monomania infects the unfortunate historian who takes it into his keeping. The idea of a 'psychoanalytic map' is unendurable in a world of Oedipal travel.[48] If Barzun's irascible tone in *Clio and the Doctors* is any indication (or Elton's tone in the Cook Lectures, or Gay's tone in *Freud for Historians*), even the most modest excursion into historiographic justification and explanation must be approached defensively, inasmuch as the very excursion violates the prime directive to push on into history regardless of doubt, regardless of fear. It is no wonder that attempts to articulate conventional historiographic procedure are felt as frustrating, for it is a procedure which, working negationally, cannot nonetheless afford to take

---

[47] Collingwood, *The Idea of History*, 228.   [48] Gay, *Freud for Historians*, 32.

the next step into assessing what its own negational predispositions might mean; like any discourse, it is fraught with contradiction, but unlike other discourses it is not equipped with the means
to accommodate them theoretically or otherwise (a religious
apprehension might adjust to contradiction in one way, a deconstructionist intuition in another, a logical positivist in another, and
so on). Thus Barzun's attempt to set up 'history' as an intact
system, separate from the vagaries and excesses of quanto- and
psycho-history, leads always to distinctions that collapse, comparisons that seem invidious, and contradictions that fragment;
his argument for free-flowing narrative is subverted because his
own narrative is troubled by its engagement with inalienable
contradiction.

From a meta-textual point of view, this disturbance coming
from within historiographic assessments of themselves is hardly
surprising, for one knows that such assessment will be felt as a
displacement of a primary relationship with external reality –
history – into a far less straightforward relationship with *language*
– criticism (and *felt* as such regardless of logical or methodological
qualifications). As Barzun says, 'This imagining or imaging of past
reality is the point of history: the evident supplies the historian
with images to communicate.'[49] From outside the expectations of
conventional historiography this distinction between reality and
the language that bespeaks it would lose much of its force, for any
enterprise that professed to gather, deploy, and evaluate information, textual and otherwise, would be considered as engaging
primarily in the limitations and freedoms of critical discourse,
narrative shape notwithstanding. From this perspective the historian, no less than the literary critic, is under an obligation to
interpret object texts, to extrapolate evidence in the form of quotes
and paraphrase, and to repeat in various incremental ways this
evidence within his own text. The balance he creates is in fact
strikingly similar to that of the literary critic: as Gay says,
'Historical narration without analysis is trivial, historical analysis
without narration is incomplete.'[50] He sustains the same burden of
reconstruction, with the same obligation to minimize distortion
while embedding salient details within his own master narrative:
he runs, in other words, the risks of the literary critic but with what

[49] Barzun, *Clio and the Doctors*, 55.
[50] Peter Gay. *Style in History* (New York: Basic Books, 1974), 189.

he insists are higher stakes because he perceives himself not only to be the monitor of real events but the arbiter of their reality in past and present time.

Doing history, telling it through narrative, is a way of sustaining a fantasy of productive action; indeed, it is a way of being an Oedipal hero, regardless of the exigencies that underlie one's actions, because it promotes action over indecisiveness and champions determinacy over nihilism or effete despair. Talking about doing history invites a world of trouble. To recognize the contradictions critically is not only to stop *doing* history, it is to threaten to stop history, to bring men out of an oedipalized commitment to the necessity for decisive action into effeminacy. Thus Elton's unreserved contempt for theory as both the cause and the effect of having entertained unmanly doubt, promoted obfuscation, and glamorized frivolity.[51] Conventional historiography senses that to yield to complicated thinking is to promote its miseries and seductive pleasures over productive, historic action; it is to prepare the ground for all the egregious effeminacies to which postmodern man is heir: doubt, irony, deconstruction, playfulness, nostalgia, retrogression, despair. To speak critically, and to acknowledge that one is speaking and thinking critically, is to acknowledge one's residence within a language system. Whether or not this awareness is carried to the level of an explicit theory of critical discourse, it will be felt as a retreat from 'history' into words.

Critical thinking – the assessment of what has previously been thought, said, and written about a subject – affords its own rewards and punishments, but in giving up the fantasy of linguistic autonomy available to lyricism or fiction it gives up one significant source of pleasure; and in giving up conventional historiography's fantasy of a relatively unmediated relationship with material, historical 'truths' it gives up another. It is a mode that by definition situates itself between narrative and speculative dialectics, and in so doing threatens any illusion of a pure continuity. Narrative, on the contrary, awakens the redemptive spirit. LaCapra writes:

Narrative provides – in a displaced way – on the level of story and events what speculative dialectics provides on the level of theory and concept. In

---

[51] Elton, *Return to Essentials*, 29.

related but non-identical fashion . . . both traditional narrative and speculative dialectics seek a redemptive, revelatory unity, totalization, or closure – a making whole again. The pattern or paradigm is one wherein a circular but progressive journey or circuitous quest seeks an end that recapitulates its beginning on a higher level of insight and development ... In a secular sense, one has a quest for the redemption of meaning and for a form of justification – a higher identity. In religion, an original state of innocence (Eden) gives way to a fall (original sin) that is overcome through a redemptive act (the coming of a messiah), and one is born again. In narrative, a beginning gives way to a middle whose in's and out's, up's and down's, are made sense of in a concordant ending. In speculative dialectics, identity gives way to difference that is overcome in a higher identity. Wholeness is broken through alienation and suffering that are transcended in a higher and greater wholeness.[52]

Critical activity, felt as a kind of stoppage, may be subsumed into the flow of narrative as long as the historian keeps himself relatively undistracted, his fantasy of a primary engagement with material evidence intact, but this repression of the critical within narrative cannot survive the importation of a foreign conceptual scheme. Thus conventional historiography knows that, by definition, psychohistory cannot work, because it binds itself to an external discourse as if it were itself not sufficient to the task at hand. The historian knows intuitively that this Oedipal failure is predetermined, because he is more than ordinarily sensitized to the difficulties of carrying out history in the face of conceptual distractions, and moreover, this particular conceptual scheme of psychoanalysis is *exactly* the sort of valorized introspection, ambiguity, and unknowability that halts narrative in its tracks. Either way it is used, psychoanalysis is trouble, for if it is deployed in it full technical complexity it will subvert narrative energies completely, and if it is used narrativistically it risks taking on the sexy particularities of case history.

Yet, if conventional historiography's disposition toward the performance of manly activity reveals itself unequivocally in its repudiation of psychohistory, psychohistory, ironically enough, proves its affiliation with historiography proper in its own attitude toward the technical language of psychoanalysis and in its persistent capacity for failure. Gay's position relative to the use of psychoanalytic language in historiography is representative, as it asks for a thoroughly informed but undoctrinaire – i.e. non-

[52] Dominick LaCapra, 'The Temporality of Rhetoric,' *Chronotypes*, 122.

technical – assimilation of psychoanalytic insight. His representative success story, E. R. Dodds' *The Greeks and the Irrational*, is a telling choice for many reasons; 'a model of what psychoanalytic history can be,' it nonetheless uses Freud, says Gay, in a 'thoroughly-informed and shrewdly sympathetic . . . wholly undoctrinaire' way. Gay goes on to say, 'Standing back from his suggestive analysis of how Greek culture moved from shame to guilt, Dodds emphatically declared his independence from psychoanalysis: "I do not expect this particular key, or any key, to open all the doors. The evolution of a culture is too complex a thing to be explained without residue in terms of any simple formula, whether economic or psychological, begotten of Marx or begotten of Freud."'[53]

And indeed, it seems unanswerable as to whether *The Greeks and the Irrational* means itself to *be* psychohistory or actually is psychohistory; certainly Dodds' own disclaimer is borne out within the book which, with the exception of a few highly qualified paragraphs on the Oedipus Complex (what else?), makes few explicit gestures toward psychoanalysis.[54] By Gay's definition, insightful analytic gestures need not be explicit – indeed, only by virtue of their full assimilation back into the river of history-telling do they prove the full, oedipalized maturity of the historian who writes. But his distinction between the serendipity of talent and the methodological finesse of the analyzed historian suggest that even an initiate might be fooled into taking native insight for psychoanalysis; 'I am not,' Gay says, 'disputing, or in any way minimizing, the capacity of a competent, unanalyzed historian to grasp the ambiguities and complexities of historical situations or the mysterious mixed motives of historical actors . . . But the perceptions of such a historian are, as it were, intransitive; they depend on the accident of individual talent rather than the ministrations of a dependable psychology.'[55] This gnosticism is appealing but problematic; certainly, the problems of intentionality become exceedingly complex here, as the continuum between the unanalyzed and the thoroughly analyzed is marked by infinite gradations of insightfulness that the unanalyzed subject may leap over in one grand intuitive moment. Early on in *Freud for Historians*, Gay quotes himself as saying, 'all

---

[53] Gay, *Freud for Historians*, 40–41.
[54] E. R. Dodds, *The Greeks and the Irrational* (Berkeley: University of California Press, 1951), 47.   [55] Gay, *Freud for Historians*, 32.

history is in some measure psychohistory,' with the disclaimer that 'psychohistory cannot be all of history'; yet this begs the very crucial questions by which one would discover the distinction between insight and psychoanalysis.[56]

Barzun and its other opponents notwithstanding, psychohistory resists the very analytic systems it employs by returning them as much as possible to ordinary language, and this gesture is perhaps the clearest signal of all regarding conventional historiography's virtually deterministic stake in the Oedipal game. For psychohistory inevitably proves what conventional historiography implies: that history must be narrative, that it must be carried out in full, manly confidence, expressed as if it were the case regardless of one's underlying timidities, doubts, and qualifications. Psychohistory is hoist on the petard of its own unbreakable affiliation with the rules of the brotherhood; it tries to assimilate the language and thinking of psychoanalysis into itself and it loses the power of both modes. If it speaks psychoanalytically in any sustained and serious way it makes its psychohistorical points at the expense of its own fidelity to narrative and to non-technical language, and if it does not use the terms and analytic procedures of a discourse that is, after all, extremely subtle and complex and specific, then it cannot be said to be doing psychohistory. Committed to many of the same methodological and epistemological assumptions as conventional historiography, psychohistory has full access neither to the exhilarating intensities of high theory nor the equal exhilaration of fiction and poetry. And yet, driven by Oedipal imperatives, it could not be otherwise; it can neither yield to the full authority of psychoanalysis nor can it impose the full authority of history. This double failure in psychohistoriography reveals that full performative strength is an act of the will, the Oedipal contract always by definition not quite complete; conventional historians sense this to be a secret too dangerous to be betrayed.

Psychohistoriography attempts the impossible, given the terms by which it senses that it must proceed, because to accept any named external system, metaphysical or psychoanalytic, as one's legitimizing narrative is to give up one's claim to history. The poet or the philosopher who is not bound to common speech may

[56] *Ibid.*, x.

translate psychoanalytic terms and insights back into metaphor, and in so doing shift the energy of such terms into another register of power. The analyst whose audience licenses a thorough deployment of technical language may, as Freud's work so potently illustrates, subvert generic imperatives and destabilize existing structures of discourse; if Freud's psychoanalytic writing tells an old story, it is sameness with a difference. The historian committed to ordinary language and the idioms of a more conversational style finds himself, often by explicit ideological choice, either in the realm of dead metaphor or approximating the language of the realist novel while eschewing the novelist's freedom. Pulled toward story-telling, where character takes shape within the generous space of a world whose ideas of human nature derive from myth and poetry and so elide the localized frameworks of psychoanalysis or Marxism or any other more narrowly articulated 'monotheistic' system, the psychohistorian must give up a crucial part of his own narrative freedom. Psychohistorians are often so preoccupied with being neither fish nor fowl, neither too fancy or difficult for common speech nor too novelistic, that their texts collapse both structurally and tonally into bifurcations that reflect this ambivalence. The psychobiographies are full of such schisms, as they frequently claim a specific psychoanalytic orientation and then, for the sake of standard narrative procedure, consign analysis to separate chapters or to paragraphs so weighty with stolid analytic summations that they act like boulders in the narrative stream. The Schreber biographies that intermittently yield narrative control to the father's voice allegorize this dynamic, but the general dissatisfaction with psychohistory as a genre (as opposed to an idiosyncratic and fairly small collection of psychoanalytically astute histories) suggests that it is more than merely recalcitrant convention that keeps the form from taking a firm, canonically rich place within historiography proper.

It is a consummate irony that the very discourse designed to elaborate upon the determinisms of the Oedipus Complex is the means of revealing the thoroughly Oedipalized nature of conventional historiography. The relationship between psychoanalysis and historiography exposes the joints of historiography's insistence upon a narrative carried out in the language of butchers and bakers. Psychoanalysis formalizes Oedipal terms, but it also licenses a discussion of them. In so doing it takes a system of behaviors whose inertial energies were monumental: everything worked to make Freud's formulation seem compellingly true because the system was already fully developed, weighted with history, adorned with literature. Indeed, Oedipus *was* history, the embodiment of a movement through time and space that must be pursued despite everything. The very language of western philosophy was tailored to the Oedipal myth and tuned to the Oedipal fantasy. The image of the journey had long ago become an inescapable metaphor for a man's progress through history; the *Bildungsroman* had by the late eighteenth-century already done the picaresque one better, and made spiritual progress – 'character – inseparable from historical, remembered, assimilated and transformed progress through time and space. As Lyotard says, 'The popular stories themselves recount what could be called positive or negative apprenticeships (*Bildungen*): in other words, the successes or failures greeting the hero's undertakings. The successes or failures either bestow legitimacy upon social institutions . . . or represent positive or negative models . . . of integration into established institutions. Thus the narratives allow the society in which they are told, on the one hand, to define its criteria of competence and, on the other, to evaluate according to those criteria what is performed or can be performed within it.'[57]

The Oedipal man is on a road to wisdom: 'the pattern or paradigm is one wherein a circular but progressive journey or circuitous quest seeks an end that recapitulates its beginning on a higher level of insight and development. (Hence the significance of the image of the upward spiral in Hegel and others.)'[58] In this story, a man has to do what a man has to do. But conventional historians are unnerved, because Freud stopped to *talk* about it: he might just as well have started a quilting club or a kaffee-klatsch. History has to shut its eyes to all sorts of things if it is to proceed; historiography must narrativize in the face of multiplicity, lost evidence, too much evidence, falsified documents, plagiarisms, hyperboles, and lies, as must we all. But psychoanalysis, in forcing the issue of the Oedipus Complex, raised the unthinkable possibility that said Complex is not 'natural,' not inevitable, not anything but historically rigged and immensely potent, a fantasy just like

[57] Lyotard, *The Postmodern Condition*, 19–20.
[58] Conkin and Stromberg, *The Heritage and Challenge of History*, 57; LaCapra, 'The Temporality of Rhetoric,' 122.

any other, only one designed to facilitate the manly work of running the world.

The frightening thing is not that of being threatened with castration, apparently. Apparently it is *not* being threatened with castration that is the scary possibility. Not to worry about it, one way or the other, would be, one way or another, not to be man, with or without penis intact. History tells us this, but not because it wants us to know it. Not because it believes this to be the case. History tells us this in the same way that Schreber tells us about paranoia, delusion, and madness, which is to say that its truth is, like Schreber's, double. Proceeding by one honest conviction regarding the truth, telling that truth in as responsible and sincere a way as possible, it may be seen as the code by which a meta-truth emerges. The Schreber paradox, a most delicious irony for those of us already within the asylum walls.

5

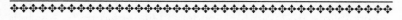

Conclusion

'Finnegan, begin again.'

After such knowledge, what forgiveness? Think now
History has many cunning passages, contrived corridors
And issues, deceives with whispering ambitions,
Guides us by vanities. Think now
She gives when our attention is distracted
And what she gives, gives with such supple confusions
That the giving famishes the craving. Gives too late
What's not believed in, or if still believed,
In memory only, reconsidered passion. Gives too soon
Into weak hands, what's thought can be dispensed with
Till the refusal propagates a fear. Think
Neither fear nor courage saves us. Unnatural vices
Are fathered by our heroism. Virtues
Are forced upon us by our impudent crimes.
These tears are shaken from the wrath-bearing tree.
                                              'Gerontion,' T. S. Eliot

Concluding Homily

Eliot's lessons on history are told by an old man in a dry month, waiting for rain, his house a decayed house. 'I am ... /,' he says, 'A dull head among windy spaces,' thinking, he says, 'Thoughts of a dry brain in a dry season.' Gerontion: he is the antithesis to our metamorphic, catastrophic Schreber, as he figures forth in his desiccated rationality certain logical conclusions about the limits of knowledge and the inevitable failures of faith. Schreber, home to hosts of delusions, seems bursting at the seams and under constant assault, in the throes of a spiritual and bodily invasion by higher powers. Gerontion, though, is the quintessential Westerner, the lapsed believer whose meager venereal economy is now invested in the fantasy of the landlord Jew, squatting on the window-sill of his decayed house under a windy knob. This old man resents his loss of faith, complains about living in a wasteland where 'Signs are taken for wonders.' His rented body/house is draughty, and even its ghosts are long gone. Passion, and the Passion are only memories: 'I have lost my passion: why should I need to keep it / Since what is kept must be adulterated?' he says, 'I have lost my sight, smell, hearing, taste and touch: / How should I use them for your closer contact?' He can speak to us about history, because in some utterly indisputable way he *is* one figure for our history, Grandfather Time, diachrony to materiality's synchrony.

But too, there is History, Clio, the poignant, potent virgin, and no chrone: 'She gives when our attention is distracted / And what she gives, gives with such supple confusions / That the giving famishes the craving.' Here we are, in it, this history of ours, every minute of every day. But to *enter* her, really, to *possess* her, really, seems an endless impossibility, because the iron-clad conditions of her availability are that one always be too distracted to take her, until after the fact of her exit. The poet's license allows him at once to confess and to universalize this dilemma of the real, the stuff of which history is made; lyricism's powers of subjective universality can enforce, perform, and refute the paradox by which the 'realness' of material existence can only ever be experienced artifactually. Gerontion, historian, implies one truth about how realness cannot *be* within time (even as Eliot's lyric potency translates this loss into a kind of gain): 'The tiger springs in the new year. Us he devours,' but that which may be remembered has *not* consumed, and is not, therefore, so much real as it is historical. Only Schreber, madman, can speak throughout his ongoing devourment. The lyricist, speaking for himself alone and outside the imperatives of historical 'truth,' may mimic Schreber's condition of chronic revelation, working by paradox and with all of the considerable, intricate doubleness language affords. The lyricist can complain lustily that what History consents to give, she gives with such supple confusions that one is perpetually wakened to unsatisfied appetite; he may, as does Eliot, splendidly, powerfully broadcast himself as victim to this appetitive cycle, repetitive but diminishing, each refutation a wearing down until the last hard time comes when the old man will 'stiffen in a rented house.' The poet can, more or less, have his cake and eat it too, inspired by loss to lament, inspiredly, the loss of inspiration. The historian, Oedipal artisan, is committed to a less devious effort of recuperation.

Perhaps recognizing this inevitable evasiveness, standard historiography makes a virtue of necessity, declaring Clio a lovely virgin and then invoking the manly value of virile moderation (desire coupled with self-control and appropriate abnegation); this is a continence that is reified in historical narrative, a discourse neither so self-indulgently desirous as lyric poetry nor so straight-laced as plain exegesis, and it is a simple reticence that psychohistoriography, by definition of its subject-matter and focus if not also by definition of its infiltrated syntax and diction, is felt to violate. Yet psychohistoriography also works to contain its sense of history's perpetual running away; its fantasy of psychic gravity – a dense interiority where nothing is ever fully lost, nothing finally unrecoverable – rescues *something* from the intuition that History cannot be fully present but exists only as past and future. History, says the poet, 'Gives too late / What's not believed in, or if still believed, / In memory only, reconsidered passion': responding to this shared frustration of muted receptivity, psychohistoriography situates history's rise and fall ontologically, a fast-running stream of consciousness troubled by the backward pull of the unconscious. Psychohistoriography sees itself as not, after all, so different from conventional historiography in its procedural response to this sense of somehow having been teased by history and is thus all the more hurt by the brotherhood's dismissive or angry responses. It too narrativizes in the face of confusion, ambiguity, and unverifiability, and it too works to bring language down from the theoretical heights and into the warm flow of history. Viewed from outside, its major difference from conventional historiography may seem its willingness to formalize a shared bereavement even as it provides the system – psychoanalysis – by which its sense of history's quotient of loss might be retrieved for the greater good of humankind.

For both conventional historiography and psychohistoriography the very fantasy (acknowledged or repressed) of a satisfactorily completed Oedipal transaction betrays a fundamental anxiety about history's subordination into any of the various metaphysics of ordering by which materiality is tied to a system of meaning. But conventional historiography cannot forgive psychohistoriography for so clearly displaying the site of the original wound, for articulating and, worse, for inevitably performing the multivalent responsiveness called forth by history's agile evasions. At the level of articulated and applied content, psychoanalytic theory provides a code whereby the implicit heroism of a self-imposed, self-aware continence will always, under the revealed compulsions of Oedipal necessity, *also* be translated as a combination of bravado and abjection in the face of desire (mother-love, castration, the whole can of worms). Anyone who acts knows that the heroism of public responsibility, however it is conceived, discovers itself only as it acknowledges the fact of its insistent repudiation of its own private necessities: it is 'manly,' or 'heroic' – the stuff of which history is made – precisely because it is not easy but difficult, 'natural' only as it reveals through travail the hidden determinisms of the naturally heroic soul. For the public man in history, then, the problem is not so much in the fact of apprehending such ambivalence, which is human nature after all, and the source, ultimately, of heroism. The problem is in the fact of psychohistoriography's willingness to talk about that which should remain – which, if it is to hold its place as a marker of successfully deferred hysteria, *must* remain – tacit.

Whether this reticence comes from an excess of anxiety or from a sufficiency of self-reliance, conventional historiography is the more successfully oedipalized in that it chooses to work within a tradition whose boundaries it will test but not, finally, violate; this oedipalized intuition whispers that psychohistoriography does not quite meet the requirements for full, initiated membership in the guild because, whatever its regard for historiographic proprieties, psychohistory is still in its essence an acting out, if not an acting up. Convention senses that psychohistoriography *performs* its resistances and capitulations with all the crafty resilience of the hysteric whose symptoms are at once evidence of superabundant control and failure of control. 'What's thought can be dispensed with,' says Eliot, 'Till the refusal propagates a fear': repression will out if history gives itself 'too soon / Into weak hands.' The semiotics of manliness measures its conformation against the ideals of the purely tacit and the intelligently laconic; and historiography, because it must be voluble, materialistic, detailed, feels itself as more than ordinarily susceptible to the womanish pleasures of gossip and self-revelation. Compelled to an acquisitive circumstantiality and a carefully intensive evaluation of specifics, historiography must maintain a decorum of containment and prudent selectivity. Psychohistoriography is felt to display a symptomatology of encoded self-revelation, handing 'history' over to the very psychic determinisms it would use to illuminate specific men and events; its very preoccupation with psychic complexities seems resonant with personal anxiety, as if certain non-oedipalized energies, unallowable, have resurfaced. So conventional historiography hears the psychoanalytic explanations themselves as confessions of incapacity. It hears the 'jargon' as evidence that historiographic self-control is being eroded from the inside and that such refusals as are necessary to manly action are being spent into a language that performs its own betrayal. By these terms, psychohistory undermines its own performative virility by talking in terms of the desires it knows cannot, by psychoanalytic definition, be fulfilled. No guts, no glory.

This psychohistoriographic anxiety could explode the whole Oedipal charade by which men and history are synonymous words against which 'woman' and its multiple synonyms may be said to come up at least five to eight inches short. A thoroughly oedipalized intuition says that the Rube Goldberg complexities of psychoanalysis, with its authoritative claiming by means of the 'Unconscious' of its own impotence, are so many acts of a purely passive aggression. If conventional historiography were willing, and able, to psychoanalyze its contempt for psychohistoriography (and it is precisely this failure/refusal that is the point), it might argue that psychohistoriography speaks with bravado within the comforting explanatory systemics of the psychoanalytic project, while it whispers abjection in its inability to synthesize psycho-analytic discourse into historiographic narrative without either being taken over by force or giving up almost all psychoanalytic specificity and language. By implicating history in the unconscious and in determinisms like the Oedipus Complex, the psychohistorian betrays himself to more masterful story-tellers as not quite fully oedipalized, still more talk than action, more psychic analysis than story. The guildworker must resist locating 'History' in this particular interiority: here, psycho-spatial reality opens like an abyss at one's feet, a bottomless place where history spends itself to nothingness. In this particular rabbit-hole, the limits of the rational prohibit fully conscious control even as the unconscious engages in covert operations.

And yet: the love–hate relationship between conventional historiography and psychohistoriography feels very much like two brothers fighting, their differences based on an inviolable kinship. One can spot 'theory' a mile off; quanto-history, at least in its ideal conception, is a different beast entirely from narrative history; but if, as LaCapra points out, even Elton, objectivist, and Carr, 'relativist,' are brothers under the skin, 'mutually supportive parts of the same larger complex,' psychohistory manifests itself with all the power of twinship.[1] For both conventional historiography and psychohistoriography, history is the blade-thin severance inside that oxymoron, 'human nature'; it is a kind of ritual scarification, the place where the Oedipal wound seals 'human' and 'nature' in a new bond of responsible manhood, a smooth ridge of the social, the active, the political. Historical psychoanalysis, psychoanalytic history: this is a fantasy that, by virtue of its affiliation with historiography, has already accepted the Oedipal contract to play by the already-written rules, and as such it stills the anarchic twitch beneath psychoanalysis' putative composures.

As against the historian, the theoretician or the poet might brave the Oedipal threat and experience the contradictions within psychoanalytic theory that can make the analyst/analysand giddy, foolish, Orphic, Whitmanesque. More than that, and more significantly than that, the theoretician or the poet is licensed to celebrate the *fact* of this contradictoriness as in itself the value of psychoanalysis. Slavoj Zizek, in exploring intellectual and political responses to the 'practico-therapeutical absurdity' intrinsic to psychoanalysis' simultaneous imperative to demolish and to strengthen defense mechanisms, exposes the range of subtlety within which one might negotiate the quotient by which psychoanalysis is said to 'normalize' its subjects. For Adorno, for example, 'What first appears as Freud's 'theoretical insufficiency' or 'conceptual imprecision' possesses an inherent cognitive value, since it marks the very point at which his theory touches the truth.'[2] Within a system committed both to the goal of reinstating

[1] Dominick LaCapra, *History and Criticism* (Ithaca: Cornell University Press, 1985), 137.

[2] Slavoj Zizek, *The Metastases of Enjoyment: Six Essays on Woman and Causality* (London: Verso, 1994), 13.

the capacity for drive satisfaction and to the goal of enhancing continence (this pushmi-pullyu beast of continent virility is not by any means a new formulation) there is an 'unbearable "contradiction,"' but Adorno maintains that it is *exactly* here in the contradiction itself that the value of psychoanalysis lies. As it reproduces 'the fundamental social antagonism, the tension between the individual's urges and the demands of society,' it can perform itself as an antidote to the Oedipal narcosis that dreams itself as fully integrated, more than almost a man.[3]

But historiography, conventional and psychoanalytic, must necessarily perform a textual and exegetical paradox that is akin to what Zizek calls 'repressive desublimation' ('the triumphant archaic urges, the victory of the Id over the Ego, live in harmony with the triumph of the society over the individual'[4]). Famously, it abjures all responsibility to the domestic, the Ego at home, belly full, hen-pecked, and worried about the bills; indeed, domesticity is the unhistorical, implicitly positing itself as changelessness or, the same thing, as all small change of an utterly trivial sort (cooking, eating, coitus, defecation, childbearing, house-cleaning, etc.). Conventional historiography and psychohistoriography concern themselves instead with those larger movements – historical – that prove a virility whose continence is self-imposed. 'Why now?', the question one must ask to begin history, implies some breaking-point from the norm. Yet, as this historiography narrativizes extremities whose factual status as 'history' allows for a total suspension of censoring exclusivity, it brings them into harmony with a socialized ideal; the flow of history, the past teaching the present, salve the very atrocities and excesses and foibles they figure forth. 'Repressive desublimation': this could be the banner under which Manhood walks in history, were it not for the fact of its being a condition whose terms cannot, by definition, be known from the inside.

'Manhood' is unthinkable without its first stepping out of anarchic singleness and/or domestic assimilations into history, but, in a fierce Catch-22, manhood cannot enact itself fully as long as it is locked within its historical awareness. As Nietzsche says, 'man can only become man by first suppressing this unhistorical element in his thoughts, comparisons, distinctions, and con-

---

[3] *Ibid.*, 13.   [4] *Ibid.*, 16.

clusions, letting a clear sudden light break through these misty clouds by his power of turning the past to the uses of the present.' 'But,' he goes on, 'an excess of history makes him flag again, for without the veil of the unhistorical he would never have the courage to begin. What deeds could man ever have done if he had not been enveloped in the dust-cloud of the unhistorical?' A man in the throes of passion is dangerous: 'His whole case is most indefensible; it is narrow, ungrateful to the past, blind to danger, deaf to warnings, a small living eddy in a dead sea of night and forgetfulness.' And yet, and yet: 'And yet this condition, unhistorical and antihistorical throughout, is the cradle not only of unjust action, but of every just and justifiable action in the world. No artist will paint his picture, no general win his victory, no nation gain its freedom, without having striven and yearned for it under those very "unhistorical" conditions.'[5] 'History,' the condition for socialized humanness, is also the limit that heroisms must exceed; 'no fact that is a cause is for that very reason historical,' says Benjamin, 'It becomes historical posthumously, as it were, through events that may be separated from it by thousands of years.'[6] Historiography, which tells as much as it can discover of what is useful to the task at hand, desublimates the stuff in Id's full bag of tricks at the same time it represses its power.

'Extremities,' by virtue of their having been assimilated already before the fact into the discourse of rise and fall, are simulacra, and the (psychoanalytic) history that lays them out, by virtue of its being real history, can only simulate psychoanalysis. There are many ways to speak of this censored garrulousness whose oxymoronic energies both hide and betray libidinal truths while editing a text whose Variorum sits, closed but at hand. Eric Santner, for example, talks of 'narrative fetishism' in 'History Beyond the Pleasure Principle' – 'the construction and deployment of a narrative consciously or unconsciously designed to expunge the traces of the trauma or loss that called that narrative into being in the first place.'[7] But however one psychoanalyzes it,

---

[5] Friedrich Nietzsche, *The Use and Abuse of History*, trans. Adrian Collins (Indianapolis: Bobbs-Merrill Co., Inc.), 8.

[6] Walter Benjamin, 'Theses on the Philosophy of History,' in *Illuminations: Essays and Reflections*, ed. Hannah Arendt, trans. Harry Zohn (New York: Schocken Books, 1968), 263.

[7] Eric Santner, 'History Beyond the Pleasure Principle,' in *Probing the Limits of Representation: Nazism and the 'Final Solution'*, ed. Saul Freidlander (Cambridge: Harvard University Press, 1992), 144.

history, historically considered, is meant to be redeemed as therapeutic, with *therapeutic* defined within the Oedipal constraints that define well-being in terms of the well-made, non-hysterical, non-feminized man. For to get history *productively* out, to transmute the full, unexpurgated, messy story into the narrative quietudes of historiographic language and procedure, is to reinforce and to perform the Oedipal excision of extremisms. As Hayden White suggests, 'traditional historiography has repressed the indeterminacy of the sublime.'[8] A controlled amputation, it circumcises a more disruptive and ongoing acting out.

Clio bemused

History as history is history in history: one can only stutter out the problem, hiccough a semantic puzzlement whose terms interlock to guarantee that history *will* repeat itself, if not circumstantially then at the least as an idealism of type. So no matter how one slices it, conventional historiography and psychohistoriography share a fundamental commitment to a past that, if it is to be deployed as history, cannot be deployed psychoanalytically. Or not really, anyway, with 'really' suggesting the same nearly liminal distinctions that one makes between philosophy and history of philosophy, history and philosophy of history: it is not so much that psychohistory is given to analyzing dead and paper people – that, as Peter Gay says, Clio just lies there on the couch – as that *history* itself is given over to death and effigy. History has its stone feast with monuments, its pieties the assumptions of a rational humanism whose limits are, within predictable variables, always defined before the fact as consonant with certain traditional forms of good behaviour, synthetically inclined. To some extent, it must always both speak to and *perform* a resurrection into memorial propriety: fact becomes History only posthumously.[9] In history, thoroughly fallen into knowledge from the Edenic ingenuousness of spontaneity, one is under the imperative to unpack everything already there and to have nothing to do with what isn't. 'A historical phenomenon, completely understood and reduced to an item of knowledge, is, in relation to the man who knows it, dead,' says Nietzsche, 'for he has found out its madness, its injustice, its blind

---

[8] From 'The Politics of Interpretation' (1982), discussed by Friedlander in the Introduction to *The Limits of Representation*, 7.
[9] Benjamin, *Illuminations*, 263.

passion, and especially the earthly and darkened horizon that was the source of its power for history.'[10] But psychoanalysis itself (the thing rather than the idea of the thing) is, to use Frost's image for poetry, like ice skittering across a hot griddle: it rides on its own melting.

When pushed, as in historiographic work on the Holocaust, to confront the limits of conventional expectations about representation, about sanity, about rationality, about evil, one discovers the limit conditions of history's capacity to assimilate and recuperate its own preoccupation with death. 'I do not think that conventional techniques, which in certain respects are necessary, are ever sufficient,' writes LaCapra, 'and to some extent the study of the Holocaust may help us to reconsider the requirements of historiography in general.'[11] History is not equipped to speak when there are too many dead for any lesson, and no sense to be made, for the Oedipal fantasy is based on a precise economy of loss and gain, sacrifice and recovery, killing off and reproducing: it presumes the decency of moderation and the capacity for guilt. 'As flowers turn to the sun, by dint of a secret heliotropism the past strives to turn toward that sun which is rising in the sky of history,' says Benjamin.[12] But if, as Geoffrey Hartman says in *Bitburg in Moral and Political Perspective*, 'The Holocaust acts as an eclipse of the *imago Dei* (of the God in whose image man is said to be created)', this eclipsing of God the Father threatens to be a final solution to the Oedipal dilemma, whose regenerative insistence on itself is based on the metaphysics of this particular solar presence – the Father-God.[13] An antithesis to any Final Solution, History's slaughters must be articulable through the Oedipal pedagogies that teach loss as salvational (as History itself is always in the process of being lost).

In its telos of productive, comprehensible, pedagogically valuable death, history offers itself as a perpetual answer to that classic question, asked through history with less pathos but the same ingenuous guile with which Bloch begins *The Historian's Craft*:

---

[10] Nietzsche, *The Use and Abuse of History*, 11.
[11] Dominick LaCapra, 'Representing the Holocaust: Reflections on the Historians' Debate,' in *Probing the Limits of Representation: Nazism*, 110. See, too, Dominick LaCapra, *History, Theory, Trauma: Representing the Holocaust* (Ithaca: Cornell University Press, 1994).   [12] Benjamin, *Illuminations*, 255.
[13] Geoffrey H. Hartman, ed. *Bitburg in Moral and Political Perspective* (Bloomington: Indiana University Press, 1986), 4.

'Tell me, Daddy. What is the use of history?' This is an economy that the absurdist excess of the Holocaust puts very much to the test. If, at heart, Oedipus' story is the most efficient way of rationalizing (our) individual deaths as comprehensible – and even tragic – in the ongoing, historically, socially, politically freighted scheme of things, if History is an amelioration for mortality, then the Final Solution threatens to return suffering and death to the meaninglessness of the purely inexplicable. Or, even worse, it threatens to expose 'enlightened humanism' as something like a mass hallucination, a psychotic break suffered under the unbearable counterweight of archaic desire. It makes Kant's formulation in 'Response to the Question: What is Enlightenment?' – 'Enlightenment is humanity's exodus from its self-imposed immaturity' – seem more than ordinarily fraught with wishful progressivism, as *Bildung* reveals itself through the dark glass of the Holocaust as bound up in a dependence on death more necrophiliac than memorial.[14] Historiography predicates its assessments of the past on the past being history, its ghosts suitable for illustrating the current lesson of the day. But, as Adorno says, 'National Socialism lives on, and to this day we don't know whether it is only the ghost of what was so monstrous that it didn't even die off with its own death, or whether it never died in the first place – whether the readiness for unspeakable actions survives in people, as in the social conditions that hem them in.'[15]

History, no stranger to barbarians, nonetheless measures itself by the distance it keeps from them, and from the women, children, animals, madmen, and brutes who fall under barbarism's auspices. History is the most polite of fictions, for it, unlike novels or poetry or political speeches or pornography, claims as its first order of business the real, important 'real'; and unlike philosophy proper it commits itself to supplying the materials for, if not also the actual telling of, a story. Walter Benjamin conveys the precisely oxymoronic nature of historiography's restitutions and amnesias even as he also conveys the meta-textual implications of this trope of paradoxical reconciliation: 'There is no document of civilization which is not at the same time a document of barbarism.'[16] As

---

[14] Quoted in *Ibid.*, 114.
[15] Theodor W. Adorno, 'What Does Coming to Terms with the Past Mean?' in *Bitburg in Moral and Political Perspective*, 115.
[16] Benjamin, *Illuminations*, 256.

Vincent Pecora shows, Benjamin's aphorism resonates in the context of National Socialism so that its own most superficial and least ironic reading – that the exigencies of 'civilizing' (the) barbarians will always also have been violent – supplies the irony on which the complexity of his observation rides.[17] For, ironically, the civilizing stories historians tell will have been told within the amnesias and predispositions of a cultural identity more or less contaminated by the political power in which it is immersed. The historical document itself is, artifactually, also a 'document of barbarism,' of taking over, pre-empting, and excising; in Habermas' reading, for example, Benjamin 'was thinking of the "public use made of history by national movements and nation states in the nineteenth century."'[18] Pecora is reminded more globally that civilizing recuperations – historical and textual – performed under the auspices of enlightenment humanism necessarily repress the barbarisms of colonization and exploitation by which the well-made man is brought into power.

Benjamin's statement, then, may be used to articulate many levels of this recognition: that any document of civilization is also a document of barbarism. But in the Oedipal dispensation, whereby the barbarism of incestual impulse *precedes* and thus legitimizes civility, the balanced interdependencies within Benjamin's formulation can only be realized intellectually, in parts, or epiphanically, as an ephemeral, gnomic whole. At best one can think of this overlay of documents as palimpsestic, with the document of barbarism overwritten by that of civilization, the first a discarded frustration that compels the next, more comprehensible attempt. History's genteel barbarism is most difficult to apprehend, as it colonizes under polite threat of the knife that prunes for civility's sake. A thoroughgoing intuition that the document of civilization – i.e. history – *is*, always, also a document of barbarism may not be possible within history but only at its very limits, for, as Benjamin says, 'this barbarism taints also the manner in which [the document] was transmitted from one owner to another' (he himself would work to combat this contamination through a historical materialism that takes as its task 'to brush history against the grain').[19] Perhaps, and who is to say for certain, it is only possible

[17] See Vincent P. Pecora, 'Habermas, Enlightenment, and Antisemitism,' in *Probing the Limits of Representation*, 157.   [18] *Ibid.*
[19] Benjamin, *Illuminations*, 256–57.

to stand at these limits as the Other from which Oedipal decorum takes its warnings.

In the Oedipal system whereby barbarism is the blessing from which civility springs, there must be men to make and, equally essential, there must be others who prove the rule of manhood by virtue of their failure to rise to the occasion of it. Externalized, this impulse invents or discovers adversaries, who may then be engaged with all the ferocity allowed within Geneva Convention rules. Elton, in *Return to Essentials*, is only more specifically combative than most when he takes up the sword against the likes of Stephen Greenblatt and Hayden White, citing examples to stand as warning 'that in battling against people who would subject historical studies to the dictates of literary criticism we historians are, in a way, fighting for our lives.'[20] The Oedipal fantasy of manliness is not prepared – cannot be prepared – to anticipate a Holocaust, because its own barbarisms are always felt in the service of civility and it cannot conceive of barbarism unadorned.

Which means, of course, something quite thoroughly sinister: that even those who carried out the Holocaust could not know the fact of their own criminality, a nightmare of unknowing that, paradoxically, will only matter finally to those most immune to these very beguilements of evil. Within this perpetual fantasy of righteous rage and causal logic (how else to justify killing the father?), Ernst Nolte's infamous question becomes inevitable: 'Did the National Socialists, did Hitler carry out an "Asiatic" action perhaps only because they regarded themselves and their kind as potential or real victims of an "Asiatic" action? Was not the Gulag Archipelago more original . . . than Auschwitz? Was not the "class murder" of the Bolsheviks the logical and factual *prius* of the "racial murder" of the National Socialists? Was it not a scientific mistake to focus on the latter and neglect the former, although a causal nexus is probable?'[21] Adorno speaks in the context of his assessment of Germany's failed 'reprocessing' of the past in a way that may only be understood within the Oedipal dispensation that

---

[20] G. R. Elton, *Return to Essentials: Some Reflections on the Present State of Historical Study* (Cambridge University Press, 1991), 39–42.

[21] Ernst Nolte, 'Vergangenheit, die nicht vergehen will,' *Frankfurter Allgemeine Zeitung*, 6 June 1986, quoted by Dominick LaCapra in 'Representing the Holocaust,' in *Probing the Limits of Representation*, 113.

ensures its truth: 'Fascism, basically, cannot be deduced from subjective dispositions.'[22]

Thus it is in the acute responsibilities of Holocaust historiography that historiographic exegesis makes itself most patently felt not only as insufficient to, but as complicitous in, the barbarisms whose stories it tells; here the ameliorations of narrative are themselves often felt as yet another enactment of the helpless nullification goodness suffers when it seeks on its own terms to expose and repudiate absolute evil, a reification, one more time, of the capacity to be surprised by, and thus vulnerable to, the unheroic banality of malice. Silence, if it could be certain of speaking, seems to some the only enormity sufficient to this particular task, and, failing that, there are historians who would supply the starkest 'most literal *chronicle* of the facts of the genocide' as the means of attaining something like 'authenticity and truthfulness.'[23] Moral purpose, Oedipal rectitude, as if its need for converts has hunted out and exposed those most vulnerable, seems somehow the necessary dupe of a less rule-bound rapacity, a sort of Judas goat that leads its own way to slaughter.

So from the limit condition of its imbrication within the possibilities of thinking a Final solution, Oedipal historiography is asked to face – as we are all asked to face – the question of complicity. It is probably fair to say that usually even the racist – or perhaps especially the racist – enjoys his fantasies of resistance and revenge within the comforting foreclosures of some law by which he might mask his cowardice or ambivalence as necessity. Tweedledee and Tweedledum battling, the Oedipal warrior conquers by mutual consent that the threat is past. He enjoys the thought of repressing an Asiatic other whose capacity for rampant licentiousness is paralleled only by his own virile continence. Eliot puts this fantasy of threat rather bluntly, the traditional figure of lyric inspiration – the bird – settling on his sill, hunched and raven-like, in the form of 'the Jew' as if to say that this dark and exotic other must be there to bring the question of history into the light of day: 'the Jew squats on the window sill, the owner, / Spawned in some estaminet of Antwerp, / Blistered in Brussels,

---

[22] Adorno, 'What Does Coming to Terms with the Past Mean?' in *Bitburg*, 124.
[23] See Hayden White, 'Historical Emplotment and the Problem of Truth,' in *Probing the Limits of Representation*, p. 44, as he speaks of Berel Lang's position relative to narrative.

patched and peeled in London.' This egregious moment in 'Gerontion' exposes Eliot's near-compulsive need to scapegoat his own venereal impulses, a confession he makes himself in the free-associational next line, 'The goat coughs at night in the field overhead'; it also, I think, betrays the secret of the Oedipal pact, which cannot write its vision of order – of history – without some gargoyle roosting just barely inside its line of sight. Poe's rusty raven croaking 'Nevermores,' the Other goads men into passion through what is felt as an unsettling mimicry of humanness.

The Oedipal story is the safe haven from which to remember, or at least to fantasize, the ahistorical necessities of strong passion: passion, for a woman, for a theory – however it is hypostasized it is desire unconditional, with absolutely no memory of death. And no knowledge of death means no history. 'If the man of action, in Goethe's phrase, is without conscience, he is also without knowledge: he forgets most things in order to do one, he is unjust to what is behind him, and only recognizes one law – the law of that which is to be.'[24] The ordinary ones of us can speak of this fantasy of pure desire only from within the conditions of history, for only the beasts as we make them up in our heads embody such 'happiness' over time. A man may ask the beast, '"Why do you look at me and not speak to me of your happiness?" The beast wants to answer – "Because I always forget what I wished to say"; but he forgets this answer, too, and is silent; and the man is left to wonder.'[25] To be 'unjust to what is behind,' to recognize only one law, 'the law of that which is to be,' would be an absolute manifestation of the death of God, the Father. For it is only within a system of metaphysical necessity that 'the law of that which is to be' can emerge already socialized. What rough beast, indeed, would come slouching toward Bethlehem if men were able to project themselves as the law of desire?

History, of all things, knows the dangerous seductions of this unmediated projection of self, as it proves in its romance with heroes, those men who can suspend the normalicies of the Oedipal in moments of high crisis and stride forth unabashed by the past. But history defines them as heroes only by virtue of their lapses back into sanity; otherwise they become Schreberians, defined retroactively within history's Oedipal telos as having somehow, at

---

[24] Nietzsche, *Use and Abuse of History*, 9.   [25] *Ibid.*, 5.

some point, gone native/mad/feral, Kurtz in the jungle. History thus hypostasizes its own dilemma in its fascination with heroes, and it provides for its own comfort and old age in the eternal, wave-like motions of their rising and falling fortunes. For one cannot *be* an historian and a hero at the same time, if heroism constitutes itself in moments of unhistoricality whose mediation in time always occurs after the fact. And if the historians cannot be heroes, heroism's ontology is in the enduring fact of its necessary evanescence: even heroes can't be heroes for long, as the sisyphean slide into history enforces heroism by making it so hard to keep intact. Heroes are pulled down into history, putting their pants on one leg at a time, and little wonder. For the Oedipal warning system elaborates itself endlessly; it is by now a net of history so densely woven as to feel inescapable except in moments of madness (Sophocles writing 'history' of sorts, from a genealogy, of sorts, spilling over into literature, to metaphor, to poetry, spilling over into Freud's system of naming: it is myth, history, poetry, psychoanalysis, an itinerary that takes one as if fated to the designated spot).

History writes history: when conventional historiography claims the right to, and the necessity of, the language that butchers and bakers speak, it makes a fairly accurate claim for a universal, oedipalized 'ordinariness' as the medium in which spectacles and upheavals and heroisms are written even as it works to create its audience as worthy listeners. If the terms of this claim to ordinariness are disputable, its significance is not, as it performs the 'history' of a certain, historically legitimated version of humanness that makes 'hero' visible on this level horizon. It performs a synthetic humanism that seems – that may even be – utterly representative of a basic, indisputable, common type, one that would extend to most of the unrepresented others, one feels, if the mechanisms of identification were only broadened. It condones normalcy; it is permission granted not to act the hero. And maybe this is, in fact, 'history,' which is to say that its humanistic expectations and definitions are true. Maybe it is also good in that it embodies a figure whose capacity for compromise exists only by virtue of its innate idealism. How can one know?

But there is a less regenerate reading as well, for it could be, too, that this level ground from which heroes rear themselves up into the sublimity of an action that, by definition, must be climactically terminal, is a vast cemetery filled not only with fallen heroes but with the mass graves of Others. ('There is no document of civilization which is not at the same time a document of barbarism.') It is not, perhaps, irresponsible to say in the context of questions of Holocaust historiography, that these Others have long been emblematized in the figure of the Wandering Jew – Oedipus (un)fated – whose diasporic identity guarantees that he will always stand as surrogate for whatever anxious miscegenetic fantasy is playing in a particular place and time. (Adorno speaks of the pointlessness of organized acts of friendship between young Germans and young Israelis as a way of 'coming to terms with' the National Socialist past: 'For this sort of activity depends too much upon the assumption that anti-Semitism essentially has something to do with Jews and could be combated through an actual knowledge of Jews.'[26]) Djuna Barnes, in *Nightwood*, writes something like an Oedipal riddle:

for the step of the wandering Jew is in every son. No matter where and when you meet him you feel that he has come from some place – no matter from what place he has come – some country that he has devoured rather than resided in, some secret land that he has been nourished on but cannot inherit, for the Jew seems to be everywhere from nowhere.[27]

Barnes' own ambiguous position relative to this Semitic metaphor is, of course, part of the riddle itself, reifying as it does the assumptions it asserts. But her lyricism may be taken as apposite to the Oedipal myth: 'the step of the wandering Jew is in every son,' whose Oedipal homecoming must, then, be a solution to this voracious, wandering 'Jewishness.' Heroes and historians cannot be 'everywhere from nowhere,' and their tight interdependency constitutes a virtual guarantee that some other will always be found out.

Heroes such as history has defined them is what makes Nietzsche's definition – 'ungrateful to the past, blind to danger, deaf to warnings, a small living eddy in a dead sea of night and forgetfulness' – Nietzschean. Which is to say that history creates the truth by which 'Nietzschean' becomes recognizable, persuasive, and seductive as a metonymy for the escape from history, and in so doing guarantees that it – history – will survive as the

[26] Adorno, 'What Does Coming to Terms with the Past Mean?' in *Bitburg*, 127–28.
[27] Djuna Barnes, *Nightwood* (New York: New Directions, 1961), 7.

great dustheap of necessarily fallen, failed, worn-out, or misbegotten transcendents. One thinks of Schreber again, the man with the messianic destiny, and how his madness takes the form of an acute recognition of how such heroism can only sustain itself as the condition of being eaten away; his metamorphic hallucinations – his sense of organs disappearing, of others melting into the beds in which they sleep – resist the truth of heroism's climactic impermanence even as they prove him to be mad. And his alternative filling out into womanliness and pregnancy – his lapses into the pleasures of voluptuousness – posit themselves as a relief from the cannibalistic gnawings of his heroic responsibilities; but even as they also prove him to be mad, these changes mark the unequivocal shift from heroism to capitulation.

Conclusion

There always comes a point in the (academically publishable) critical enterprise when history reasserts its pre-eminence, even if disguised in a rhetoric of disavowal. Enforcing itself as the distinction between *Being* (a fundamentally ahistorical immediacy allowable to, for example, lyricism) and *doing*, history asks that the text put its money where its mouth is and provide some answers. It says, 'So what do you intend to *do* about these problems you have raised?' Never mind that this is the most classically Oedipal question of all, predicated from within its own defining assumptions that an answer is a thing, transferable, a token of exchange within an Oedipal economy. Never mind that without answers there could be no history, no justification for wading in with the question, 'Why now?' 'The proof,' history says tartly, 'is in the pudding.' History, the story of the real, reasserts itself as composed of discrete, artifactual elements, so indisputably material that they are immune even to the various curatorial interventions of narrative. It takes the Johnsonian line and suggests that, theory notwithstanding, the real can always prove its existence as a tangibility by falling on one's head or tripping one up, and with a badly stubbed toe. Sticks and stones will break your bones, history says, with a definitiveness even the most performative language will fall far short of.

But protesting too much, these anxious and defensive responses to the insubstantiality of theory necessarily rise out of a discipline acutely sensitized from within by its own felt distance from the active heroisms of which it speaks. The story of rise and fall and rise and fall counts heroism, completely atemporal during its brief duration as a form of freedom from history, and it counts history; heroism can only be conceived from *within* history and only be legitimized after the fact as something other than madness *by* history. This compound of abjection and pride, whose allegory is Oedipus, is powerfully regenerative, working both to sustain itself and to co-opt alternative modes by drawing them into its system of competition and conflict. There is no place within this dynamic for an indeterminacy that rests without resting its case; one may play a multitude of epistemological, philosophical, and textual games inside a *telos*, which is to say that indeterminacy is not necessarily felt as inadequate or unfinished unless it fails to wrap itself up in the end.

This instinct for conclusion may be an ontological given among a humankind whose most denied, repressed, negated, present, acknowledged, and irrevocable certainty is death; the Oedipus Complex may be a natural product of the unconscious, so fundamental a necessity as to constitute humanness all round. The need to finish up may be truth, and if so then History, which embodies this apprehension of conclusion and conclusiveness, is as it claims to be, also Truth. In other words, history may, in its most generalized methodological expectations regarding evidence and in its responsibility to the documenting of meaningful human interventions in the material world, perform itself as a humanism written according to a historically/ideally/metaphysically accurate ontological measure. Then again, and who knows, history may be an endless elaboration on a fundamental error, in which 'human' is covered over by something that comes to be called, through the devices of negation, 'humanism' ('I am not an animal').

The questions as I have posed them throughout this book should be taken, then, as divested of any idea of a final solution as regards the truth of the matter. An oedipalized reading will say that I have proceeded negatively, dismantling a subject without offering viable alternatives. But this would be the case only if I were dismantling (or attempting to dismantle) the subject, and only if I held apart some alternative metaphysic of my own. In my mind, this project is not so much an interrogation as a meditation or a mediation; its value, or lack of it, is in its performative capacity to engage its readers in a kind of responsiveness. And inasmuch as I consider this engagement itself to be of mutual value as it happens, I also posit it as something like the 'answer' that brings this text to teleological order. How to write history – to tell truth? The answer is, in its broadest possible and least ideological or programmatic definition, psychoanalytic, which means that it presumes the value of the interminable ongoingness of analysis, psychic, critical, and historical, that it recognizes its complex connectedness with the material past it seeks to document, that it is wary of its own capacities for negation, denial, and repression, that it would work to listen as well as to speak, and to hear beyond the fatedness of Oedipal determinacies. And, recognizing all this indeterminacy, it would write history anyway.

This is an order of the most flexible sort, and rather than answering the question of how best to *do* historiography it simply defers it. Viewed from within oedipalized anxieties, this order would hardly be worthy of the name, and it would display itself as having achieved something less than closure, less than 'manhood,' less than heroism, showing itself to share the relatively un-bounded, amorphous, and indeterminate territory of the Other. It is an ordering that argues a subtlety of adjustment almost Jamesian in its preoccupation with a mostly internalized pro-gramme of response (Henry James – another sissy); it says that every move that translates into action must arise from the intricacies of a multivalent consideration of alternative readings and possibilities. On the one hand, and seen within the Oedipal dispensation, this may threaten manhood with passivity, inaction; it will seem to warrant the same scorn, and for similar reasons, that historians like Elton have heaped on the deconstructionists, the theorists, and the feminists, as it is felt to clear the way for a lazy nihilism too effeminate even to be attractively Nietzschean. But on the other hand, it may be the quintessence of what has been wrongly encoded under the term, 'manhood,' in that every written word of history that arises from this extraordinarily dense histori-cal field becomes an act of heroism. Which is to say nothing more or less than that as it writes it knows itself to be in the moment of *acting* outside the safety net of history, even as it also knows that it is perpetually falling back into the perspectivism, uncertainty, and bewilderment inevitable within the flow of such a swollen stream.

The latter possibility escapes the bipolar disorders generated under the duress of metaphysics, for working within this ratio of thoughtfulness to response can count as dualism only under the metaphysical fantasy that, given enough evidence, it will become possible to know unambiguously that one is doing right (a different thing from actually doing it). The metaphysical fantasy unites history and heroism in some future apotheosis, a time when truth is known and the hero is no longer, at the moment of his gesture, outside of the history that has always before been able to legitimize him only after the fact. (I think that this fantasy helps explain the iconographic power of Bloch's *The Historian's Craft*, for here in this one text, finally and absolutely, is heroism embodied, the last words of a man taken out to be shot for his beliefs.) I would say instead, and without the regret, the triumph, or the sense of loss that conventional historiography would say it, that writing history and writing about historiography are two irreconcilably different projects, that theory is not history, that philosophy is not history, that psychoanalysis is not history, and that when these things become history ('the history of . . .') they cease to be theory, philosophy, or psychoanalysis. I would, then, suspend the historian's calisthenic efforts to find ways to include 'good' cross-over efforts. (Barzun's footnote to the phrase 'philosophy of history' is a good example: 'This accepted term is not to be confused with philosophic discussions of the nature of historical knowledge, such as one finds in Burckhardt, Dilthey, Collingwood, Arthur Danto, and others, including some of the "philosophers of history" in the other sense of the term.'[28]) I would say that this surrender is precisely the solution to historiography's self-defined sense of its own discrepancy with the manly heroes it documents; for this would mean that history-writing does not defer heroism but enacts it, as it leaps into history, into narrative, into truthtelling, and into the salvational even as it recognizes before the fact its own unendurable uncertainty.

For pragmatically semantic (and semantically pragmatic) reasons having to do with the problematic issues of genre, I would, then, ditch the fantasy of assimilating theory into any history-writing that also wishes to remain semiotically intact as immediately recognizable, historically situated history, while at the same

---

[28] Barzun, *Clio and the Doctors*, 119.

time I would work to stretch the boundaries of what counts as 'narrative' or 'story-telling.' And this is not, to my mind, a capitulation or a compromise. Only by working reflexively *within* the predominate hierarchy does one see the possibilities of a fully inflected narrative history as somehow a failure relative to the truth-telling possibilities (whether conventionally defined or in post-structuralist terms) of another mode. The scientistic prejudice whereby story-telling is felt as less true, less important, less of everything that goes toward fact-finding, the materialist distaste for that 'whore called "Once upon a time,"' can only arise where there are declared or covert fantasies of 'objective' universals.[29] Indeed, only *within* these assumptions can one situate 'narrative' and the connotatively laden term 'story-telling' as if, in the realm of that neutral thing 'prose,' there is a possibility for uncategorical distinctions regarding truth values. And when narrativizing is embraced or dismissed as somehow the most 'natural,' basic, and harmless kind of communication, it remains unexamined and Oedipally potent. When apprehended as a sort of transparency on which one marks the stuff to be projected, narrative prose can be expected to *perform* already written foundational expectations.

It is best to remember that story-telling is not merely pleasurable, in the laudatory or pejorative senses that ascribe to it a power of transport less intense than, but in its own way as effective as lyric poetry. One should keep in mind that it lends itself to providing a seductively normative alternative to the easily perceived extremisms of heroism and the sublime. This is particularly the case in a discipline whose own awareness of its rhetorical strategies has been systematically repressed under the fantasy of a stripped down, 'plain style.'[30] Unexamined, or defensively sentimentalized as the foundation on which butchers and bakers and historians mold and cut their materialist, everyday wares, its brand of dispossession can become generic, an invasion of the Oedipal body-snatchers. As LaCapra says, 'Transference may be blindest when disciplinary or subdisciplinary boundaries and protocols of research become the foundations for a self-enclosed frame of reference that induces the methodological scapegoating –

---

[29] Benjamin, *Illuminations*, 262.
[30] See Hayden White, 'Rhetoric and History,' in *Theories of History*, Hayden White and Frank E. Manuel (Los Angeles: William Andrews Clark Memorial Library, 1978), 4–7.

the exclusion or reduction – of phenomena and perspectives that cannot be fully adjusted to it.'[31] Self-deprecation and bravado will dog the historian every step of the way as long as the inertial force of the already-written remains unnoticed and unchecked.

Paradoxically, many of the historians most sensitive to narrative effect turn away from story-telling, either as an explicit theoretical/methodological choice or because of a more or less repressed intuition that history-writing of the easily recognizable sort is not as authoritatively felt as is metahistory. For metahistorical analysis, far from being vitiated by philosophical and psychoanalytic discourses, is enriched by them; and of equal significance, is enriching of them as well. 'How to confront the limitations of a documentary model without simply converting all history into metahistory . . . is a complicated issue,' says LaCapra, 'but one the historian is increasingly forced to face':[32] metahistory is, in its way, a profound relief from the felt contradictoriness of history-writing. Historians who have turned to various modes of theoretical assessment seem fated to move from the enterprise of writing history to the enterprise of writing about writing history, as if, once having fallen from historiographic innocence, there is no going back. There is as a consequence an immensely rich body of post-structuralist work on historiography and an unresolved split between those who write history, those who write about historiography from various post-structuralist positions, and those who write about it out of recuperative responsibility.[33] It is as if the historian's punctilious regard for evidence and his uneasy rela-

---

[31] Dominick LaCapra, *History and Criticism* (Ithaca: Cornell University Press, 1985), 73.   [32] LaCapra, *History and Criticism*, 21.

[33] As a very limited bibliography, see, for example, Sande Cohen, *Historical Culture: On the Recoding of an Academic Discipline* (Berkeley: University of California Press, 1986); Saul Friedlander, ed., *Probing the Limits of Representation: Nazism and the Final Solution* (Cambridge: Harvard University Press, 1992); Jurgen Habermas, *The New Conservatism: Cultural Criticism and the Historian's Debate* (Cambridge University Press, 1989); Geoffrey Hartman, ed., *Bitburg in Moral and Political Perspective* (Bloomington: Indiana University Press, 1986); Lynn Hunt, *The New Cultural History* (Berkeley University of California Press, 1989); Hans Kellner, *Language and Historical Representation: Getting the Story Crooked* (Madison: University of Wisconsin Press, 1989); Dominick LaCapra, *History, Theory, Trauma: Representing the Holocaust* (Ithaca: Cornell University Press, 1994); Jean-François Lyotard, *Heidegger and 'the jews'*, trans. Andreas Michel and Mark Roberts (Minneapolis: University of Minnesota Press, 1990); Mark Poster, *Foucault, Marxism and History: Mode of Production versus Mode of Information* (New York: Polity Press, 1984), and Poster, *The Mode of Information: Poststructuralism and Social Context* (Polity Press: 1990).

tionship with metaphysics push in one direction or the other, but cannot, historically speaking, push both ways. The theoretically inclined historian becomes a theorist, the psychoanalytically inclined historian devotes himself to recognizing and recovering the endless permutations of one's transferential relationship with history, other historians, and other texts. There is no easy back and forth between writing about writing history and writing it, and this in large part, I think, because historians, like most of us, are conditioned to apprehend narrative prose as a more primitive, less intellectual, less 'masculine' mode than the philosophic or the theoretical.

Perhaps only a non-historian, by definition already capable of the considerable promiscuities associated with literature and literary criticism, could imagine a historian capable of both a commitment to the necessity and value of theory and a commitment to the necessity and value of narrative: this would be the historian who combines theory and history, psychoanalysis and history, not in the same texts but concurrently. This will not happen as long as even the most self-aware, analytically astute writers remain within a conceptual scheme that subordinates story-telling to some fantasy of attainable truth and that locates narrative only as relative to, at most in an asymptotic relationship with, more powerful, more 'masculine' modes of assessment. In *Language and Historical Representation*, Hans Kellner speaks of 'the turn to storytelling by certain prominent nonnarrative historians': 'The stories seemed to be luxury articles, earned as indulgences after the drudgery of economic, social, climatological, family, demographic, history.' 'Just to get the story *straight* is the first duty of the historian,' he says;[34] straight, as in correct, factual, straightforward, honest, and matched up to truth, and, I would add, straight as in not at all queer. Work first, then play, maybe. Story-telling, in the Oedipal dispensation, is always looking to veer off into fabrication, ornamentation, and cosmetic beguilement. But to *'Get the story crooked,'* as Kellner advocates, would be to look at 'the *other* sources of history, found not in archives or computer databases, but in discourse and rhetoric.'[35] This is a radical order, because it would mean that fundamental and sacrosanct historiographic distinctions – between primary and

[34] Hans Kellner, *Language and Historical Representation: Getting the Story Crooked* (Madison: University of Wisconsin Press, 1989), 294; vii.   [35] *Ibid.*, vii.

secondary sources, between facts and hearsay, between interpretation and reportage, between gossip (feminine) and material detail (masculine) – would come under substantial revision.

All theoretical skepticism as to sayable, verifiable truth notwithstanding, this predisposition to feminize and thus to discount story-telling (as gossip, as fiction, etc.) is so thoroughly ingrained as to be, I think, virtually ineradicable; one can only wrestle it down moment by moment through the self-imposed exigencies of what I am loosely calling psychoanalysis. One must be willing to give up the fantasy of an unimpeachable authority, which is the same thing as giving up the fantasy of power that is fully oedipalized 'manhood.' 'After such knowledge, what forgiveness?' asks Eliot. How can there be absolution, when the distinctions between heroism and history, men and women, the historian and his paramour, Clio, erode? As Bonnie Smith shows in 'Gender and the Practices of Scientific History: The Seminar and Archival Research in the Nineteenth Century,' the language historians have used to speak of their historiographic research is thoroughly sexualized: archives are 'raped' by bad men, saved by archivists who see them as 'harems' of 'so many princesses, possibly beautiful, all under a curse and needing to be saved.' After penetrating these archival beauties, one might speak of becoming the 'progenitor' of new knowledge. And after a long night's work, one might return to the purely cerebral, ideal space of the seminar room, an enclosure that 'spiritualized and universalized the undertaking' after the fact.[36] In those 'mostly stag affairs' that have constituted history, a fully sexualized, responsibly oedipalized manhood has been felt as imperative.[37] And story-telling, in this venue of history, becomes a ratio of pride to abjection, the thrill of discovery always glossed by post-coital triste.

Perhaps it is no accident that one of the best examples I can give of the co-operation among modes is a book written collaboratively by three theoretically astute, feminist historians, Joyce Appleby, Lynn Hunt, and Margaret Jacob, *Telling the Truth About History*; in the genre, history of historiography, it sets out to produce a history of the discipline that accounts for its biases and that fills in the

---

[36] Bonnie G. Smith, 'Gender and the Practices of Scientific History: The Seminar and Archival Research in the Nineteenth Century,' in *American Historical Review*, 100, 4 (October 1995), 1150–76.

[37] *Ibid.*, 1151. Quoted from J. H. Hexter. Review of Mary Beard's *Woman as Force in History*, *New York Times Book Review*, March 17, 1946.

spaces that have gone unnoticeably empty. An 'old-fashioned' narrative told in classically pellucid, 'ordinary' language, the book appears to be simplicity itself, but it is a fully charged simplicity from the flyleaf on. The authors list themselves alphabetically, and the Acknowledgments begin, 'This book has been a real collaboration, and as a consequence all of the chapters express the views of all of the authors.'[38] (It is worth saying here that for obvious Oedipal reasons genuine collaborative efforts are rare among conventional historians, where the delicacies of shared authority appear variously, as in, for example, '*History*, by John Higham, with Felix Gilbert and Leonard Krieger'). From the title on – *Telling the Truth About History* written in almost comically bold-faced type – it announces an ironized vision, one that, knowing all of the arguments to the contrary by heart, sets out to write a conventional-looking history using conventional methods of documentation and research. Sensitive to issues of pedagogy, a fact revealed first in the dedication, 'To our students and our teachers,' it gives up the professorial terror tactics that keeps readers and students in their places, while it sustains a quietly persuasive authority. There are other ways, of course, than the collaborative, to write Oedipally disinclined analysis; the point is, instead, that this text is designed from the ground up to perform a less authoritarian kind of teaching.

In the Oedipal dispensation 'small heroism' is an oxymoron; I imagine it here as both good and possible in that it contains a measure of the hero's self-awareness ('Unnatural vices / Are fathered by our heroism,' says Eliot, 'Virtues are forced upon us by our impudent crimes'). It presumes self-knowledge – that which distinguishes the hero's actions from folly, arrogance, or madness, that keeps him from becoming Schreber; it assumes his apprehension that he acts always within the unbounded contingencies of history and it also assumes his equal refusal to give in to passivity and impotence. I think, given his celebration of psychoanalysis' self-contradictory energies, that this self-questioning is what Adorno has in mind when he says, 'The need for an exact and undiluted knowledge of Freudian theory is as imperative as ever. The hatred for it is directly of a piece with anti-Semitism, not just because Freud was a Jew but because psychoanalysis consists

---

[38] Joyce Appleby, Lynn Hunt, Margaret Jacob, *Telling the Truth about History* (New York: Norton Books, 1995).

precisely of a critical self-reflection that puts Anti-Semites into a seething rage.'[39] I would say that history needs psychoanalysis and all of the other tools of introspection and deconstruction; it needs feminist theory, and the philosophical, literary, and linguistic interrogations by which it may become better acquainted with its own quotient of aporia and amnesia, and with its place in the multiply overdetermined Oedipal narrative. This is not the same thing at all as saying that there can be, for example, psychoanalytic history; in fact it is the opposite of this in that it presumes the truth exactly of the conventional historiographers' assertion that the two modes are incompatible. But, clearly, the insights that theory, philosophy, and psychoanalysis may afford in thinking through and writing about historiographic issues themselves are completely compatible and, indeed, as necessary a corrective for the former three as for the latter. Suspending but not forgetting this sense of limitless contextuality during the moments of history-writing may seem the smallest of small heroisms. In my book, this is the best one can do.

[39] Adorno, 'What Does Coming to Terms with the Past Mean?' in *Bitburg*, 127.

Index

Adams, George Burton, 14–15, 17
Adorno, Theodor, 119, 148–49, 155–56, 159, 168–69
Anti-Oedipus: Capitalism and Schizophrenia, 1, 6, 70, 74, 85, 95, 97
Appleby, Joyce, *et al. see Telling the Truth About History*
Aristotle, 5, 69, 72, 76
Austin, J. L., 61, 68

Barnes, Djuna, 159
Barthes, Roland, 35, 43, 52, 53, 54, 59, 63
S/Z, 122, 125–26
Barzun, Jacques, 2, 12–13, 15, 55, 65, 68, 69, 75, 94–95, 110, 115, 118, 131–35 passim, 163
Beale, Howard K., 39
Benjamin, Walter, 50, 118, 150, 152, 153–54, 164
Bloch, Marc, 1, 32–37, 94, 112, 120, 152–53, 163
Bloom, Harold, 66, 67

Carr, Edward Hallett, 112, 148
Cohen, Ed, 93
Cohen, Sande, 119
Collingwood, R. G., 11, 21, 22, 58–59, 70–71, 83, 98–99, 102, 110, 127, 129, 131, 134

Davis, Natalie, 33–34
Deleuze, Gilles and Felix Guattari *see Anti-Oedipus: Capitalism and Schizophrenia*
de Man, Paul, 127–28

Demos, John, 30
Derrida, Jacques, 10, 34 124–25
Descarte, Rene, 122–23
Dickinson, Emily, 55, 77
Dinnage, Rosemary, 27
Dodds, E. R., 24, 138
Donne, John, 40, 69

Eliot, George, 56
Eliot, T. S., 143–44, 145, 146, 156–57, 167, 168
Elton, G. R., 19, 20, 114, 130, 136, 148, 155
emasculation, 23, 93
Emergence of Prose, The, 55–56, 72

Faulkner, William, 72, 108
Febvre, Lucien, 33–36
Freud, Sigmund, 6–9 passim, 27–28, 29, 31, 35, 42–43, 44, 51, 59–60, 63, 66, 67, 68, 73, 74, 78, 79, 80, 83–84, 85–89 passim, 90, 91, 96–98, 99–100, 101, 121, 141, 148
Frost, Robert, 2–5, 19, 23, 30, 61

Gaskell, Elizabeth, 113
Gay, Peter, 12, 15–16, 37, 64–65, 73, 87–88, 94, 103–05, 112, 125, 135, 137–38, 138–39, 151
George, Alexander and Juliette George, 25, 26
Goux, Jean-Joseph, 7

Hartmann, Geoffrey, 152
Hegel, G. W. F., 31, 72
hermeneutics, 129–31, 133

Index

DATE DUE

MAR 0 7 2000			
			Printed in USA